Sustainability Performance and Reporting

Sustainability Performance and Reporting

Irene M. Herremans, PhD, CPA

Sustainability Performance and Reporting

Copyright © Business Expert Press, LLC, 2020.

Cover image licensed by Ingram Image, StockPhotoSecrets.com

Cover and interior design by Exeter Premedia Services Private Ltd., Chennai, India

All rights reserved. No part of this publication may be reproduced, stored in a retrieval system, or transmitted in any form or by any means—electronic, mechanical, photocopy, recording, or any other except for brief quotations, not to exceed 400 words, without the prior permission of the publisher.

First published in 2020 by
Business Expert Press, LLC
222 East 46th Street, New York, NY 10017
www.businessexpertpress.com

ISBN-13: 978-1-95152-720-4 (paperback)
ISBN-13: 978-1-95152-721-1 (e-book)

Business Expert Press Financial Accounting, Auditing, and Taxation Collection

Collection ISSN: 2151-2795 (print)
Collection ISSN: 2151-2817 (electronic)

First edition: 2020

10 9 8 7 6 5 4 3 2 1

Printed in the United States of America.

To all those who want to be proud of entrusting a pristine and diverse planet to future generations for everyone to enjoy in a sustainable manner!

Sometimes it falls upon a generation to be great, you can be that great generation.

—Nelson Mandela

Abstract

As organizations tackle global challenges, the face of our businesses and our economic systems are changing to consider the interest of all stakeholders rather than just shareholders. This book provides a step-by-step approach for organizations to reap benefits from a more sustainable approach. It begins with a brief history of the development of the concept of sustainability as it applies to both performance and reporting. Implementing sustainability in an organization begins with the development of policies which are consistent with the expectations of its stakeholders. An organization's active participation in multi-stakeholder initiatives helps to align the policies with societal trends. Once the policies are developed, a management system is crucial to ensure congruence of policies with actual performance. Then, periodic reporting of performance based on well-recognized standards aids stakeholders to assess an organization's performance. It also helps stakeholders to determine if performance aligns with their expectations. Both internal and external assurances can aid in developing stakeholder trust in the organization's performance and reporting. Finally, the book concludes with a reflection on key messages and potential future actions for continuous improvement.

Keywords

sustainability performance; sustainability reporting; reporting standards; stakeholder engagement; management systems; credibility; indicators; assurance

Contents

Acknowledgments xi
Introduction xiii

Chapter 1   The Concept of Sustainability 1
Chapter 2   The Concept of Sustainability Reporting 21
Chapter 3   Sustainability at the Organization Level 39
Chapter 4   Management Systems for Sustainability 57
Chapter 5   Indicators to Report Performance 71
Chapter 6   Credible Reporting 91
Chapter 7   Assurances 109
Chapter 8   What the Future Holds 131

Glossary 141
References 149
About the Author 157
Index 159

Acknowledgments

My sincere thanks to the following people who generously supported my work on this book. Markus Selkirk helped in many diverse ways, too numerous to mention them all. In brief, Markus located excellent examples of sustainability performance and reporting for use in the book, took on research efforts to develop the time line, read initial drafts and provided insightful, detailed feedback to ensure each chapter was consistent with the identified objectives, and helped with seeking permissions. Mel Wilson and Jing Lu, both professionals in the area of sustainability, provided relevant and thoughtful comments to improve my drafts. Romaine McLeary helped with the formatting. Minh Nguyen created excellent graphics for the slide decks and figures for both the textbook and the instructor's guide. Elizabeth Romo-Rabago provided support for permissions and supplemental materials that complement this book. Tinu Chineme and Jo Mark helped with the final editing. My gratitude also goes to the many organizations that willingly provided examples and illustrations to make this book come alive. I extend my heartfelt thanks to each of you and many others who supported the development of this book indirectly but are not specifically mentioned here.

Introduction

In the words of the African Delegate from Johannesburg to Rio+10, sustainability means:

Enough—for all—forever.

Sustainability integrates the environmental and social dimensions within the economic dimension of an entity's operations to ensure sufficient resources and a good quality of life for present and future generations. To some, sustainability appears to be an enormous challenge that is too overwhelming and not worth the effort. In contrast, others are well on their way to making our world a better place for all. For example, 89 percent of business leaders say "commitment to sustainability is translating to real impact in their industry" (United Nations Global Compact-Accenture Strategy 2018, p. 11). In line with the sustainability concept, the influential Business Roundtable (BR) in the United States has redefined the role of a corporation as benefiting all stakeholders (Business Roundtable 2019), not just shareholders. This BR commitment was signed by 181 of the nation's CEOs. These businesses believe that partnerships and other collaborative arrangements are essential to address the challenges that we face. The material in this book provides an approach for working together through commitment both to sustainability performance and reporting. Performance supports reporting and vice versa.

Stakeholders wishing to grasp an organization's performance or managers of any type of entity wishing to improve their performance and make their reporting more credible will find the material in this book relevant and useful. Reporting should be a natural extension of performance not only to inform internal and external stakeholders about an entity's sustainability journey but also to learn to improve performance. Reporting has evolved and is continuing to evolve from reports that were initially called "green glossies" in the early days to current day integrated reports. Integrated reporting combines conventional financial reporting with environmental and social reporting to demonstrate the organization's value added through maintenance of its capital assets (both tangible and intangible) in the short term, medium term, and long term.

This book begins in Chapter 1 by questioning whether our current economic model is appropriate for practicing a more sustainable capitalism. It gives a brief history of sustainability along with an overview of conventional and emerging sustainability models and their strengths and weaknesses. Chapter 2 couples sustainability performance with reporting to comprehend how they are interrelated. It provides a brief history of major environmental disasters that spurred the demand for more transparency. Companies responded through various means of communicating sustainability information causing sustainability reporting to evolve over the years. Now, there is a plethora of demands for sustainability information. Many multi-stakeholder groups, including corporations, are involved in setting reporting standards and raising the bar on various aspects of sustainability and its disclosure. Chapter 3 introduces a model for a sustainable organization. Chapters 3 to 7 cover various elements of this model by providing guidance on how an organization begins its journey of continuous improvement toward sustainability. This journey starts with organizations engaging their stakeholders to determine the topics of importance (material topics) to them (Chapter 3). Once materiality is determined, the organization then develops its management systems incorporating critical policies and procedures to ensure its sustainability objectives are fulfilled (Chapter 4). Certain reporting standards help select appropriate indicators to measure performance; however, organizations should consider desired inputs, outputs, outcomes, and impacts, as well as efficiency and effectiveness in the indicator selection process (Chapter 5). Quality sustainability reporting incorporates essential qualities, such as comprehensiveness, credibility, comparability, balance, and others (Chapter 6). Although organizations generally produce one comprehensive sustainability report appropriate for all its stakeholders, they have many reporting demands that range from voluntary to mandatory, broad to sector specific. Organizations develop internal controls and undergo internal audits to reach their sustainability objectives. Some organizations choose to have certain aspects of their reports assured by an objective third party to ensure a certain degree of accuracy (Chapter 7). Finally,

Chapter 8 recaps where we have been and where we might be going. It reviews major concepts and speculates on the direction of sustainability performance and reporting for the future.

The book uses many examples and illustrations from leading-edge organizations to provide context to the material. It places the reader in the world of sustainability performance and reporting. Various learning aids are interspersed throughout the chapters to support the reader's understanding of the points of view of organizations and their many diverse stakeholders. Some of these include the following:

Sustainability in Action: Examples from organizations' actual experiences.

Reflections: Thoughtful questions or concepts that require critical thinking.

Key Takeaways: Reviews of major concepts in each chapter.

Glossary: List of terms and their definitions.

CHAPTER 1

The Concept of Sustainability

Main purpose: To comprehend sustainability as a concept: models, definitions, its relationship to capitalism, and its evolution.

Objectives: After reading this chapter, you should be able to do the following:

- Recognize that companies are rethinking capitalism to be inclusive of the concepts of sustainability and stakeholders.
- Clarify the dimensions of sustainability and the role of stakeholders.
- Identify events that helped to shape the concept of sustainability over the years.
- Compare and interpret various models used to represent sustainability.

The purpose of any company should be to make people's lives better. Otherwise, it shouldn't exist.
—Ford Motor Company, Letter from William Clay Ford, Jr. Executive Chairman Jim Hackett, President and Chief Executive Officer

Rethinking Capitalism: Sustainability and Stakeholders

We are living in exciting times as we move forward to clean up our planet and make it a better place for everyone to live. No doubt we face challenges, but as we work together to share knowledge and resources, our journey will be made easier. Our journey is one of sustainability, not sustainability as a final destination or as an afterthought, but rather sustainability as an integrated and innovative approach to the way we conduct business, referred to as sustainable capitalism or sustainable business. To begin this journey, let's review a few basic characteristics of these two concepts: capitalism and sustainability. We will then be in a position to discuss how a capitalistic system might be adjusted to serve society's needs and expectations in a more sustainable manner.

Capitalism

A capitalistic economy generally has the following characteristics:

- Private ownership of most resources through shareholder ownership;
- Competitive markets providing high-quality goods and services based on supply and demand;
- Low amount of government interference and regulation;
- Individuals working to create wealth in their own self-interest; and
- Growth and expansion through reinvestment of profits.

Sustainability

These characteristics of capitalism worked well in a very different era: one of plentiful natural resources and fewer people. However, today's capitalism needs to address societal concerns, such as climate change; air and water quality; land contamination and reclamation; scare resources for a growing population; harmful working conditions; and equal opportunity regardless of race, religion, or gender. Self-interest and low government regulation do not address these concerns well.

The capitalism of today needs to fit within today's context: one that recognizes the expectations of all stakeholders affected by a company's activities, not just the shareholders (owners). As well, companies are expected to carry out their operations while respecting their employees, customers, and communities. At the same time, they should produce products and services efficiently to conserve resources and lessen their impacts on the environment. Because the wealth in large corporations is often greater than the economies of small countries, businesses should be expected to use that wealth to solve society's problems and provide a higher quality of life for everyone.

To address society's problems, companies of today are integrating environmental and social issues into their operations to become more sustainable. A sustainable business is cognizant that a healthy environment and prosperous communities lead to a more stable and resilient world for current and future generations. Sustainability considers three dimensions that strive to include everyone:

- economic (products and services are provided profitably);
- social (all members of society share the wealth and enjoy a high quality of life);
- environment (economic and social activities should leave the planet with diverse, plentiful resources for the use by, and enjoyment of, current and future generations).

These three dimensions of sustainability are also known as the 3Ps of profits, planet, and people. Considering all stakeholders, sustainable businesses produce *profits* as if the impact on the *planet* and *people* is important as well. Even though other models of sustainability have appeared over the years, we will use this original depiction of sustainability, still very popular today, to contemplate how capitalism can integrate sustainability into business operations (Figure 1.1).

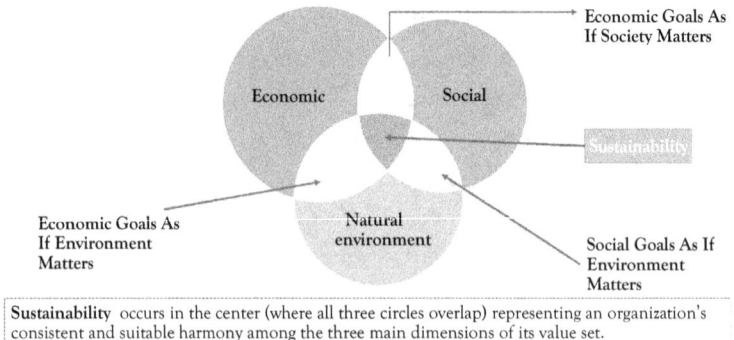

Figure 1.1 Sustainability Venn diagram model

Source: Based on Sadler (1990).

Sustainable capitalism assumes a higher purpose than just making profits. That is the reason some of the more recent models of sustainability have substituted the term prosperity for profits. Prosperity broadens the purpose of a business to benefit all members of society, not just maximizing value for the shareholders. The purpose of our economic system, and thus our businesses, should be creating value for all members of society not maximizing value for just one type of member of our society: those fortunate enough to hold ownership in our corporations through their stockholdings.

> ## Sustainability in Action: Philips and the Circular Economy
>
> *It is important to disrupt your business before someone else does. At Philips, we have started the process of fundamentally redesigning our business and our end-to-end value chains.*
>
> —Frans van Houten, CEO Royal Philips 2014, 6

Something that is sustainable is maintained, continued in existence, or kept going over the long term. The basic concept is that we need to balance these three dimensions in our decision making. Even though we often discuss sustainability in the context of business operations, every entity, whether an individual, employee of a for-profit or nonprofit organization, or a government and its agencies, must address three basic questions for each activity or project in which we engage.

- Is it economically or financially feasible?
- How does it affect (positively and negatively) the air, water, land, and other elements of our planet?
- How does it affect (positively and negatively) humans regarding their health, well-being, and quality of life?

Each dimension of sustainability has specific characteristics. Table 1.1 helps comprehend the importance of these dimensions, their strengths, limitations, and interdependencies.

Table 1.1 Characteristics of the dimensions of sustainability

Economic Dimension	Environmental Dimension	Social Dimension
Represents transactions that have economic value and can be purchased or sold in the market place.	Represents the surroundings in which we live including, but not limited to, the many ecosystem communities, their components, and relationships.	Represents the activities that occur by living in groups or communities and the way group members treat each other.
• Extracting, producing, distributing, and consuming. • Monetary value of transactions, property, or possessions. • Ease of measuring and tracking through business documents determined by markets. • Damage to environmental and social goods from economic activities (externalities) often not included in the market price unless internalized through regulations. • Therefore, many goods/services can be under-priced.	• Maintaining the balance in our many ecosystems (including air, water, and land). • Privately held resources (such as raw materials) or charges for resource use (such as water) carry a monetary amount. • Public goods belong to everyone but do not have a ready monetary value, such as the air we breathe. • Externalities (such as air pollution) are borne by the public unless a law or regulation internalizes them to the company. • Internalizing external costs follows the polluter pays principle. (Those who pollute pay for the cleanup cost, e.g., carbon tax).	• Balancing individual rights with community rights to satisfy basic human needs and improve quality of life. • Difficult to quantify and value. • Values will vary depending on regional culture and beliefs. • Examples include gender and racial equity, human rights, safe working conditions, access to education, arts, recreation opportunities, and health care. • Because social aspects are difficult to value, they often are provided through community resources or monitored through regulation.

Stakeholders

To address the environmental and social dimensions, sustainable companies engage with their stakeholders to create wealth for all of those affected by their operations. Stakeholders are classified as both primary and secondary. Primary stakeholders engage in economic transactions with a company as shareholders, creditors, employees, suppliers, and customers and are often referred to as the company's value chain. Secondary stakeholders are affected by a company's activities and consist of regulators, governments, community groups, environmental and social institutions, and members of society, to name a few (Freeman 1984). Secondary stakeholders generally do not engage in economic transactions with the company, as primary stakeholders do, but are touched by a company's activities either positively or negatively (Figures 1.2 and 1.3).

Even though the change to a more sustainable society requires perseverance and innovation, the old way of doing business (only in the

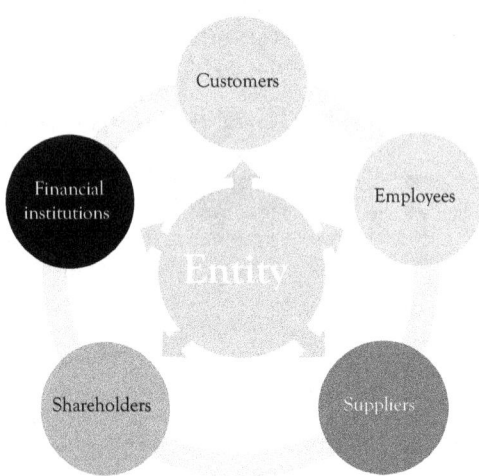

Figure 1.2 Primary stakeholders (value chain)
Source: Based on Freeman (1984)

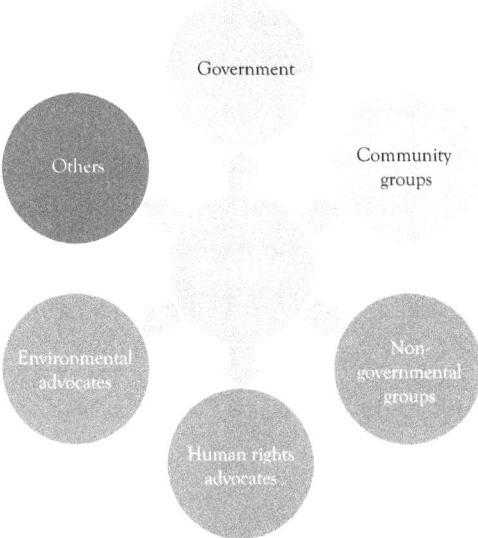

Figure 1.3 Secondary stakeholders (indirect)

Source: Based on Freeman (1984)

self-interest of the owners) will not work in a society that has limited resources to serve the needs and wants of a growing population. Therefore, when facing major global challenges (such as the elimination of poverty, a better standard of living for everyone, and the mitigation of climate change) companies that practice sustainable capitalism implement a strategy of sharing resources to remain competitive as a group or sector. The way forward is less about the *survival of the fittest* and more about *joining forces so everyone survives and prospers*. There is strength in numbers, and better outcomes can result when all are moving in the same direction.

Beinhocker and Hanauer discuss *Redefining Capitalism* in McKinsey Quarterly (2014). Considering the role of the stakeholders, they suggest that a better measure of prosperity or wealth, as well as the success of its economic system and its businesses, is the number of solutions to human problems society has produced. Consequently, rather than measuring the rate of growth by gross domestic product, a better indicator is "the rate at which new solutions to human problems become available" (p. 5). The conventional financial measures of business success such as profits, growth rates, and shareholder value are not indicators of solution generation for all stakeholders. Therefore, if an economic system and its businesses are generating more environmental and social problems than solutions for those problems, change is necessary.

Sustainability in Action: Benefit and Certified B Corps

Some corporations have concerns that solving society's problems may conflict with increasing shareholder value, given that corporations' legal responsibility is to their shareholders, not to society. Throughout this book we will study many examples of how a focus on all stakeholders actually increases shareholder value. However, to allay fears that sustainability activities may not increase shareholder value, the Benefit Corporation was created that legally allows the corporation to pursue sustainability initiatives and has legal obligations of accountability, transparency, and purpose.

Benefit Corporations may also wish to be certified, but there is no legal requirement to obtain a B Corp certification. B Corps receive their certification from the nonprofit organization, B Lab.

—Certified B Corporation n.d.

Sustainability in Evolution: Changing Expectations

To understand where we are regarding sustainability, it is best to understand how we got here. Therefore, we start with a brief history of the evolution of sustainability. There is a concept called legitimacy theory that underlies the sustainability concept and helps to understand the actions of organizations and how they must constantly change as society's needs and desires change (Dowling and Pfeffer 1975). The theory in very simple terms is this. Hypothetically, society grants a company a social license to operate as long as it produces a good or service in a form that is acceptable to society. However, the types of products and the acceptable manner for producing those products change over the years. If a company does not change as society changes, it will no longer be allowed to operate.

Reflection: Which Products Lost Their Social Licenses?

Can you think of any products, services, or practices in the past that are no longer available due to a change in environmental or social standards?

Let's look at a brief history of how the context of implicit social license has changed from 1945 to current times.

Economic Emphasis Only

During World War II (1940 to 1945), many resources were needed to support the war, leaving few resources for consumer goods. There was a shortage of consumer goods because most resources were used to produce war equipment and supplies. After the war people wanted to get on with their lives, set up their homes, and start families. When the war was over, everyone wanted a car, a refrigerator, a washer and dryer, a television set, and many other household goods that were not available during the war years.

Because of the enormous demand for products and very little capacity to produce these products (much of the world's production capacity was destroyed), consumers were willing to accept any product that was available, defects and all. There was little concern about how it was produced or, within reason, how many defects it had. At that time, companies' primary roles were to produce goods and services that consumers wanted. There was limited consideration of the role of business beyond its economic function. Organizations were deemed to be legitimate on the basis of the economic benefits they provided. If consumers did not perceive economic benefit, then the free market system based on supply and demand would deem the product unacceptable and production would be discontinued with little thought given to the environmental and social implications of the product's production process. The sustainability model looked similar to Figure 1.4 with strong emphasis on the economic dimension and little attention paid to the environment and social dimensions.

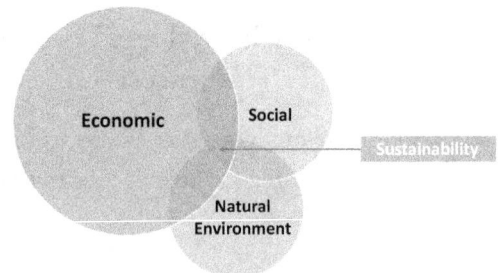

Although overlaps occur, the economic goals overwhelm the social and environmental goals suggesting the economy far exceeds the carrying capacity of the planet and does not support a quality lifestyle for everyone.

Figure 1.4 Unbalanced and unsustainable

Growing Attention to the Environmental Dimension

Later in the 1960s and 1970s, our world population continued to grow and much of the world's production capacity was rebuilt. Consumers could be selective about the types of products that they wanted to buy. Society expected goods and services that were economically beneficial without causing extreme harm to the environment. For example, Rachel Carson wrote *Silent Spring* in 1962 revealing the harm that the chemical DDT, widely used to rid agricultural crops of weeds, was causing to our bird population. As birds ate the plants that were sprayed with DDT, the shells on their eggs became very thin, causing birth rates to decline.

Growing Attention to the Social Dimension

The use of DDT also brought concern about health issues, placing emphasis on the social aspect of sustainability. Other social concerns also arose. In the 1970s factory workers fought hard with picket lines and strikes for safer working conditions and a share of the profits that they were instrumental in creating. Often corporations showed large profits, but employees' wages remained stagnant. Companies pushed employees to work harder for increased productivity as global competition got stronger. Even today, we hear about poor working conditions, often in the textile industry, that are referred to as "sweat shops."

Sustainability in Action: Quaker Oats' Social Progress Plan

Although it took most companies some time to respond to a change in their business operations, Quaker Oats, a worldwide marketer of food and beverage products (now merged with PepsiCo), approved its first Social Progress Plan in 1964. The plan contained information on a great number of social topics, such as opportunities for youth and minorities, drug abuse, and health care, among others.

—Koch (1979)

Therefore, acceptable methods under which products were produced were changing. Society now wanted products that met higher standards: economically beneficial, socially acceptable, and environmentally responsible.

While Carson is often credited with initiating the environmental movement, many individuals promoted environmental awareness at this time. In response to a changing world context and changing definitions of what are legitimate products and services, in 1983 the United Nations convened the World Commission on Environment and Development (WCED). This Commission provided an opportunity for all nations to work together to address both human degradation and deteriorating environment conditions. The document that emerged from the Commission was published in 1987 and is referred to as the Brundtland Report or *Our Common Future*. It is named after the Commission's Chair Gro Harlem Brundtland. The Commission recognized that finding solutions to our problems requires everyone's efforts. Sustainable development was defined as "development that meets the needs of the present without compromising the ability of future generations to meet their own needs."

- "Needs" refers to the basic necessities of the world's poor;
- "Limitations" refers to the Earth's resources as finite (Brundtland 1987).

In 1992 (five years later) the first international Earth Summit followed the WCED. Because it was held in Rio de Janeiro, Brazil, it was called the Rio Earth Summit. The heads of state agreed to work together to address concerns regarding climate change, biological diversity, and loss of forests. The focus was primarily on environmental sustainability. Agenda 21 was the plan for implementing sustainable development, and a Commission was created to report on performance (United Nations 1992). Early attempts to achieve goals in one dimension sometimes were perceived to conflict with the ability to achieve goals in another dimension. Through experience organizations have learned to reduce the conflict and find joint solutions, but we are all learning how to resolve these conflicts in innovative ways. Throughout the chapters of this book, we will work together to clarify how the dimensions can be harmonized by using examples from companies that are finding a better way to do business.

Sustainability Models

After the Brundtland report, the United Nations has continued to lead the sustainability movement with accords, conventions, conferences, agreements, compacts, guidance, objectives, goals, and more. Stakeholders of all types have worked with the United Nations to support the movement, which we will study in the ensuring chapters. Illustrations can help us understand the evolution of these concepts.

Venn Diagram

Even though the diagram of the three overlapping circles of economic, social and environment (Figure 1.1) is likely the most common depiction of sustainability, as we learn more about sustainability, our thinking evolves as well.

Nested Circles

Because of concern that the scale of resource use might continue to grow to outpace the limits of our planet, the nested circle diagram joined the Venn diagram as a depiction of sustainability. This model shows that the economic dimension is a subset of society, and society is a subset of the natural environment. The nested circles diagram illustrates that companies and societies must not consume resources, especially nonrenewable, outside the limits of its carrying capacity (the number of people the planet can hold without harmful destruction) and without concern for the resources needed by future generations (Figure 1.5).

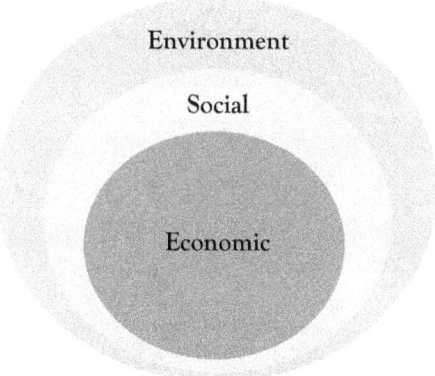

Figure 1.5 Sustainability: Nested circles

Sources: Based on Senge et al. (2008)

Millennium Development Goals

In 2000 the United Nations emphasized the social needs of people living in poverty, especially in developing countries. The eight Millennium Development Goals (MDGs) were introduced with a target date of 2015 for fulfilling the goals (see Figure 1.6).

14   SUSTAINABILITY PERFORMANCE AND REPORTING

Figure 1.6 Millennium development goals
Source: United Nations (2015)

Sustainable Development Goals

Even though considerable progress was made on the MDGs, world leaders felt that redirecting the goals into the 17 Sustainable Development Goals (SDGs) would be more inclusive. Every organization and person should take responsibility for working toward the goals most relevant to them. This approach would increase participation through a world effort with every type of entity helping: for-profit; nonprofit; governments (cities, states/provinces, and federal); government agencies; universities; civil society groups; and individuals (Figure 1.7).

With 193 countries of the UN General Assembly all working together the possibility would be much higher for accomplishing the 169 targets for the 17 goals. Even though sustainability is a continuous journey, the targeted date for reassessment of the SDGs is 2030. There is already a strong movement by companies to take on a role in achieving the SDGs.

THE CONCEPT OF SUSTAINABILITY 15

Figure 1.7 Sustainable development goals

Source: United Nations (2015)

Sustainability in Action: Unilever

The problems our society faces—such as climate change, inequality, plastic pollution and lack of sanitation—are urgent, large and complex. Change in our own business is not enough. We need transformational change to whole systems if we are to make a genuine difference on the issues that matter. That's why we're taking action on the UN Sustainable Development Goals through our transformational change agenda.

—Unilever 2019

Five Ps Model

With the expansion of the MDGs to the SDGs, the concept of the 3Ps expanded into the 5Ps, adding peace and partnerships to profits (sometimes broadened to prosperity), people, and planet (Figure 1.8) (United Nations SDG Guide 2015).

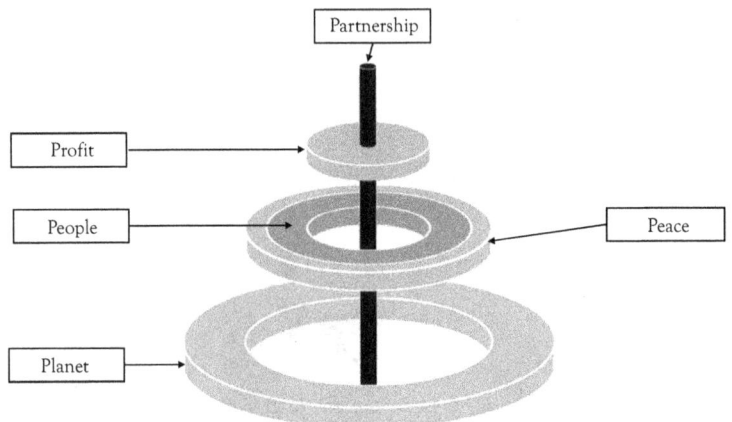

Figure 1.8 Sustainability: Five Ps

Source: Based on United Nations (2015)

Five Capitals, Value Creation Model

Although not coming out of the United Nations initiatives, one more concept is worth mentioning here (discussed more thoroughly later).

Porritt (2007) and his Forum for the Future has introduced the concept of maintenance of five capitals. The five capitals consist of financial, manufactured/built, natural, human, and social/relationship. The International Integrated Reporting Council (IIRC) added intellectual property as a sixth capital. Each capital (better defined as asset) is described briefly in Table 1.2.

The Capitals Model focuses on integrating sustainability more fully into the business model. The five capitals are similar to a statement of financial position or a balance sheet that lists an organization's resources. Then, the company engages in a number of activities or business transactions using the five capital resources. These transactions appear on a

Table 1.2 Value creation capitals model

Capital or Asset	Relationship to Sustainability Model	Description
Financial	Economic/profits	Cash and other forms of near cash to be invested in the development of other capitals.
Manufactured or Built	Economic	Material goods or assets used to manufacture or distribute product/services, such as equipment, plant facilities, computers, buildings, bridges, roads, and infrastructure.
Natural	Environment	Resources coming from the planet including air, water, and land, renewable and non-renewable that provide a flow of energy to produce goods and services.
Human	Social	People's knowledge, skills, expertise, motivation, beliefs, and spirit that are used in productive work whether paid or voluntary.
Social or Relationship	Social	Institutions or relationships that support development, manufacture, distribution, and ownership of other types of capital, such as stakeholders (either primary or secondary).
Intellectual (added by IIRC)	Economic	Brands, patents, copyright, reputation, and other forms of intangible assets flowing out of research and development, knowledge management, and innovation activities.

Based on the work of Porritt (2007) and IIRC (2013).

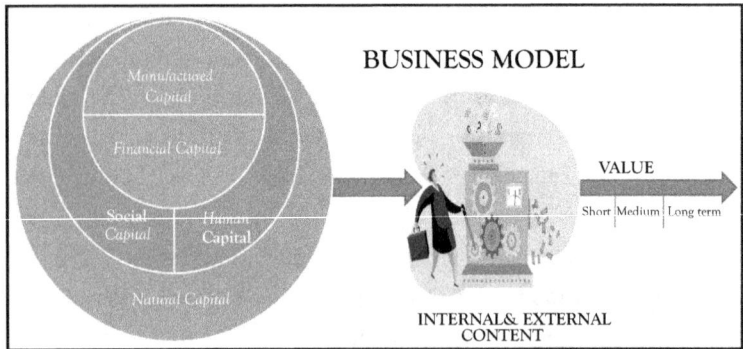

Figure 1.9 Five capitals and value creation

Source: Based on the Forum for the Future (n.d.) and IIRC (2013)

statement of operations/income statement. However, the value creation capitals model more fully classifies the value (as outputs and outcomes, either negative and positive) into short, medium, and long term for all the capitals not just financial. If positive outputs/outcomes are greater than capitals consumed in the operating process, then value is created through maintaining or providing even greater stocks of the five capitals. Figure 1.9 illustrates the concepts. Notice that all the capitals are nested within the natural capital. Therefore, the development of these capitals should not exceed the limits of the carrying capacity of our planet.

Comparison of Sustainability Models

You might be thinking that you are overwhelmed by so many sustainability models and fail to see the relationships among the evolution of the six models this chapter addressed. However, think of the models as an evolution with refinements and extensions of the original model, not as completely different models. As we have gained a greater understanding of sustainability through experience and research over the years, our models have also included these greater insights. Table 1.3 summarizes the strengths and weaknesses of each of the models to comprehend how the weaknesses in one model lead to strengths in another model.

Table 1.3 Sustainability models: Strengths and weaknesses

Model	Strengths	Weaknesses
Venn	Easy to determine the meaning of the overlapping areas: profits as though the environment and people are important as well.	Does not illustrate that society and the economy are subsystems of the environment and cannot expand beyond its carrying capacity.
Nested Circles	Illustrates a more realistic relationship of the economy and society as subsystems of the environment.	Lacks detail on the various aspects or subsystems of the three dimensions.
MDGs	Provides more explicit goals for each of the subsystems.	Tends to represent problems primarily in developing countries.
5Ps	Recognizes that sustainability is a joint effort and must be accomplished by nations (and their entities) working together peacefully and through partnerships.	Difficult to define the overlap of each of the Ps. The illustration is more complex and difficult to understand.
SDGs	Provides more explicit goals for each of the subsystems, recognizing that both developed and developing nations and their entities must play a part to accomplish them.	Gives the appearance that the goals can be accomplished separately but many are interdependent.
Five/Six Capitals	Parallels the business model and illustrates value creation as the primary objective of business and an economy. Emphasis on continuous improvement.	Not well known or understood at this time. The interrelationships among the capitals are not always evident, especially to financial capital.

Reflection: Your Personal Sustainability Model

Sustainability applies to every type of entity and every individual in our society. Although we might have the impression that our businesses create a greater impact than we do as individuals, if we accumulate the small impact of approximately 7 billion people of 2020, that creates a very large impact. Therefore, if each of us lessens our impact, together we can make a very large difference. Furthermore, we are our corporations. Many of us will work for corporations or buy products/services from large corporations. If we expect corporations to act responsibly then we ourselves must also act responsibly by choosing the types of products and services that we demand from our businesses. If you draw your three circles of sustainability to illustrate your lifestyle, what size would each of the circles be now and in the future? Are they of equal or unequal size? Why? Which SDGs do you see as most relevant to your lifestyle and how can you help to achieve these goals?

Anyone who thinks that they are too small to make a difference has never tried to fall asleep with a mosquito in the room.

—Christine Todd Whitman

Key Takeaways

- We need to rethink capitalism to include sustainability and stakeholders. Many businesses are already incorporating these concepts into their business operations.
- The basic model of sustainability considers the economic, environmental, and social dimensions. The model suggests that profits are important for an economy, but profits should not be the sole objective.
- Capitalism as practiced by organizations should be designed to solve society's problems not to create more problems.
- Companies are allowed to operate only if they have an implicit social license.
- Societal requirements for a social license evolve over time; business operations must evolve as well.
- The Brundtland Report from the WCED stirred nations to come together to determine how to address international sustainability concerns.
- As we learn more about sustainability, models depicting sustainability evolve as well. Some of the models include: Venn and Nested Circles diagrams, MDGs and SDGs, Three Ps or five Ps diagrams, and Values-Creating Capitals model.

Competition makes us faster. Collaboration makes us better.

—Author Unknown

CHAPTER 2

The Concept of Sustainability Reporting

Main purpose: To comprehend sustainability reporting as a key partner with sustainability performance.

Objectives: After reading this chapter, you should be able to do the following:

- Interpret how key events related to sustainability performance motivated sustainability reporting.
- Explain and provide examples of how sustainability reporting is an essential component in the decision-making process of the organization and its stakeholders.
- Recognize important events in the evolution of sustainability reporting.
- Identify similarities and differences in key reporting guidelines.

A big motivator for preparing a report is that improved reporting improves your performance. Sustainability reports are not there to simply communicate a message of the past to our stakeholders; they should also signal where we are headed in our future; they should drive performance improvement internally.
—Anonymous Energy Reporting Company

Reporting Progress on Sustainability

In Chapter 1 we reviewed the concept of conventional capitalism and how it must be adjusted to include recognition of the environmental and social dimensions. Our planet has limited carrying capacity (e.g., the number of human beings that it can support at one time and continue to regenerate);

therefore, as our population grows, its inhabitants consume greater quantities of resources, leaving fewer for future generations. Entities of all types, especially businesses, are adjusting their practices to create value in the short-, medium-, and long-term period by finding solutions to society's problems. In the process of finding solutions, entities are providing opportunities for everyone to share in the wealth through a better quality of life.

Thus, we are learning how to balance economic, environmental, and social values for a more resilient, long-lasting world. Embedded within the sustainability concept is the idea that a sustainable company should be the type of organization that its stakeholders want it to be, not the type of organization that only the owners or managers want it to be. Consequently, engaging stakeholders to understand their needs and desires is essential if an organization is to be sustainable.

Undertaking environmental and social activities is the prelude to reporting about them in a sustainability report. Reporting on the progress toward improved sustainability is beneficial not only for the organization's own continuous improvement but also for stakeholders to learn of its activities. Therefore, organizations create reports that provide qualitative and quantitative information about their sustainability activities. Table 2.1 gives some examples of the questions that arise in the process of internal and external stakeholders' decision making.

The sustainability report, in part, acts as an accountability document. It is one source of information for determining if the organization's activities are legitimate and whether its implicit social license to operate should be renewed. Without sustainability reporting a corporation's stakeholders are left without knowing a company's sustainability direction, what it intends to achieve, which activities have been implemented, and which challenges it yet faces. Similar to financial reporting, after a company engages in financial and economic activities for a period of time (usually a quarter or a year), it reports on its progress to its financial capital providers through its financial statements and annual report. Likewise, a company should also report how it used social and environmental resources to those influenced by or with a stake in these activities.

Financial performance reporting, based on rigorous principles, has a long history which began in 1929 spurred by the collapse of the financial markets during the Great Depression. In comparison, sustainability

Table 2.1 Sustainability reporting for decision making

Stakeholder Category	Examples of Decisions
Primary Stakeholders: Capital Providers	
Financial institutions want to lend to organizations that are not causing harm and support projects that are sustainable.	Can innovative financing arrangements, such as green bonds, support sustainability efforts? Will the company become insolvent and leave contaminated land for the public to clean up? Are projects supported through our financing causing great harm to the environment? Does funding support oppressive regimes?
Shareholders want to invest in companies that have good governance and provide a steady return on investment.	Has the company reported all environmental and social risks that could affect financial performance? Is the top management team's compensation based on performance? Does the board of directors have the owners' interests or their own interests in mind? Does the company practice strong corporate governance?
Other Primary Stakeholders	
Customers want products that will not be harmful to their health or destroy the environment.	Which products/services are safe and healthy? Under what working conditions were they produced? Can I take back, recycle, or properly dispose of the product at the end of its life cycle? Can the product be easily repaired?
Supply chain members want to deal with companies that avoid corruption and deal fairly.	Will the company deal fairly? Does the company live by its own code of ethics? Does the company stand by the quality of its products? Is the company dependable?
Internal Stakeholders	
Employees and potential employees want to be proud of their company.	Does this company have the same values as its employees? Does the company live its values? Do I, as an employee, find a good fit with this company? Will I, as an employee, find personal fulfillment?
Managers want to improve performance.	What are the risks and opportunities associated with our sustainability policies? How can achieving sustainability goals support our economic goals? How does our progress compare to our peers? Are our segments leading or lagging?

Secondary Stakeholders	
Communities want companies that will provide a good quality of life.	Does the company hire local workers and support local businesses? Does the company pay competitive wages? Does the company support sport and cultural activities? Is the company controlling pollution?
Regulators want companies to uphold the law without costly monitoring.	What types of penalties and infractions has the company incurred? Does the company have good systems to ensure compliance? Can we trust the company? Will the company work with regulators to uphold and improve standards?

reporting has a short history. Although there are some early examples, most reporting on environmental and social activities has only been around since the late 1980s. Similar to the Great Depression that motivated and improved financial reporting, several environmental disasters during the 1980s motivated sustainability reporting.

As new financial instruments and business transactions appear, financial reporting principles change to accommodate a new business context. As the financial community gains more experience with these innovations, the reporting on them improves. Sustainability reporting is also improving as more knowledge is gained about how reporting can be more useful and relevant to decision making.

Sustainability in Action: Shell

In 1975 Deutsche Shell (now Royal Dutch Shell) was a leader in sustainability reporting by providing its first Social Balance Report. It was one of the first corporations to release a report on its environmental and social performance.

Source: Kaya and Yayla (2007)

Evolution of Sustainability Reporting

As the concept of sustainability evolved (Chapter 1), sustainability reporting evolved as well. Although it is useful to conceptualize an abstract, high-level model of sustainability, organizations need additional guidance and detail to provide a relevant and useful report on their sustainability performance.

Because reporting should be connected to a plan, various institutions first developed policies or guidelines that defined acceptable business behavior. Many companies also participated in the development of these plans as they were interested in operating at a higher standard as well.

Around the same time that the World Commission on Environment and Development (WCED) produced the Brundtland Report, in 1981, the Organization for Economic Co-operation and Development (OECD) provided direction in the form of Guidelines for Multinational Enterprises (OECD 2011). The OECD guidelines and similar policies became the foundations on which companies developed their performance reports (policies are discussed in Chapter 3).

In the early 1980s as disasters occurred primarily in resource-extractive industries (such as chemical, petroleum, mining, and forestry) and manufacturing, the media were instrumental in communicating the details to the public worldwide. Therefore, companies responded by using a few pages in a separate section of their annual financial reports to convey selected aspects of their social and environmental activities (mostly in narrative form).

The debate of the economy versus the environment became heated during the 1980s, and each camp had its champions. Economically, many countries, especially developing countries, were suffering from stagnant or depressed economies while at the same time incurring huge debt burdens. Then, several disasters brought corporate practices to the forefront, which changed the focus of the debate and motivated transparency through sustainability reporting.

Bhopal India 1984 Gas Leak

- *Disaster:* A gas leak in 1984 at a Union Carbide plant in Bhopal, India killed approximately 3,800 people and permanently or partially disabled several thousand more.
- *Response*: Although the Bhopal disaster was not the only incident leading to action by the chemical industry, Responsible Care was launched in Canada in 1985 providing a set of guiding principles and a set of reporting standards.
- *Today:* The program has been adopted by major chemical companies in 67 countries (ICCA n.d.)

Exxon Valdez 1989 Oil Spill

- *Disaster*: An oil spill by an Exxon tanker near Valdez, Alaska contaminated the surrounding waters, harming both wildlife and economic conditions for the fishing and tourism industries. Incurring considerable cost to clean up the spill, Exxon's stock price dropped, and its ability to raise capital decreased. The petroleum industry experienced greater cost of regulation and restrictions on drilling, revealing the interconnection between poor environmental practices and financial health and calling into question the industry's legitimacy/social license.
- *Response*: The Coalition for Environmentally Responsible Economies (CERES) released the Valdez Principles (later renamed the CERES Principles), a 10-point code of conduct for companies.
- *Today:* About 60 companies have signed to follow the principles (Ceres n.d.).

At the time these events occurred, most companies were not ready to undertake comprehensive sustainability reporting. They did not know where to start or what to report. When they did receive signals from their stakeholders as to what they should report, their information systems were sorely lacking and did not contain the data to provide stakeholders with what they wanted. Even recently, one company tells about its challenges of reporting on water use.

Sustainability Reporting in Action

So we have lots of water activities . . . we measure, we monitor, we report, but we don't have any way to put all that together at a corporate level. To gather that information (for our stakeholders), we might invest $100,000 to answer the question so that it is repeatable . . . IT systems, training costs, and more.

—Anonymous Multinational Reporting Company

Sustainability Reporting Guidelines: Broad Based

Organizations began to realize communicating with their stakeholders helped to make better decisions and better reports. They slowly built their information systems to accommodate their stakeholders' needs. In the early 1990s stand-alone reports (separate from annual financial reports) were starting to emerge, with a strong emphasis on the environmental dimension, as it is easier to provide quantifiable indicators on environmental aspects, such as polluted air, disturbed land, and water used or contaminated. The social dimension received little emphasis, except for safety performance and charitable donations. Demands to perform in a more responsible manner came from owners of corporations through shareholder resolutions, as well as the general public.

Some of the companies, institutions, and organizations that were leaders in sustainability reporting felt standards or generally accepted guidelines would be helpful to guide their reporting, similar to GAAP (Generally Accepted Accounting Principles) or IFRS (International Financial Reporting Standards) for financial disclosure. Guidelines and standards that played an important role are identified in the next sections.

PERI (Public Environmental Reporting Initiative)

- *Initiative.* Although not well known, PERI guidelines were developed in 1993 and one of the first reporting guidelines. They were the product of a group of multinational organizations who volunteered their time to develop guidance useful in preparing their own reports and for other organizations wishing to begin reporting.
- *Supporters.* A few of the companies supporting more standardized reporting were Amoco, Dow, DuPont, IBM, Northern Telecom, Polaroid, and United Technologies. The PERI guidelines have been replaced by the Global Reporting Initiative (GRI), Integrated Reporting (IR), and other initiatives.

GRI

- *Initiative.* Starting in 1997, GRI developed reporting guidelines that were revised four times over the years, referred to as G2, G3, G4, and then Standards. In July 2018, organizations began using the Standards. Even though predominant users of the standards are corporations, many different types of entities follow the GRI Standards to some extent. GRI also offers Sector Disclosures with additional details for certain industries.
- *Supporters.* CERES (formed after the Valdez spill in Alaska), the Tellus Institute, and the United Nations Environment Programme (UNEP) joined forces to form the GRI. A multi-stakeholder group, representing a diverse collection of viewpoints, helps to develop and review the guidelines/standards periodically. They are quickly becoming the best known, worldwide standards among sustainability reporters and users (Figure 2.1).

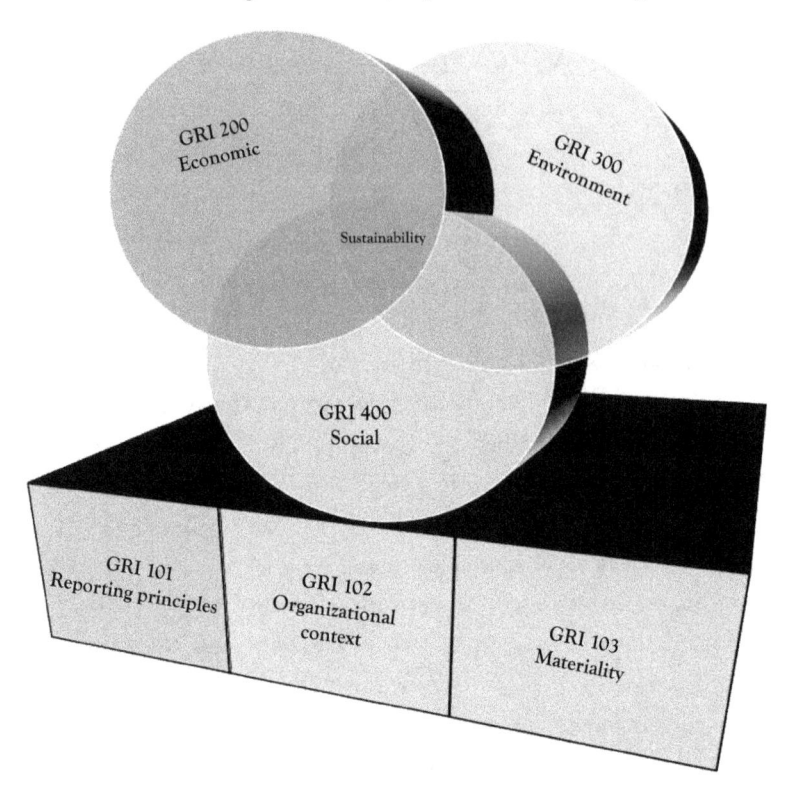

Figure 2.1 The GRI standards
Source: GRI

GRI Standards

The GRI Standards consist of three universal standards and three topic specific standards. Universal standards: GRI 101 (foundation and reporting principles), GRI 102 (disclosure for organizational context), and GRI 103 (process for material topics). Topic specific standards: GRI 200 (economic), GRI 300 (environment), and GRI 400 (social).

Standards Rather Than Guidelines?

Guidelines are recommendations that provide direction in the early stages of development of sustainability performance and reporting. In the early stages many changes in guidelines occur as organizations gain experience. PERI and GRI both started as guidelines; the GRI recently transitioned to standards after an acceptable manner of behavior had been established for quality performance and reporting. However, standards are still likely to change but not as frequently as guidelines.

Sustainability Reporting Guidelines: Specific Disclosures

More recently, a proliferation of sustainability reporting requirements from various institutions has emerged. The requirements range from broad (all aspects of sustainability) to one aspect of the environment or social (carbon, forest, water, conflict minerals, pay ratios, and more)

MDGs and SDGs. When the MDGs (2000) and the SDGs (2015) became available, leading reporting companies included their progress in accomplishing them. These goals fit nicely under the original three dimensions of sustainability (economic, environmental, and social), and the GRI Standards provide guidance on how to report on these goals as well.

IR. In 2010, the idea of integrated reporting (IR) brought sustainability reporting back to the annual report. The International Integrated Reporting Council's (IIRC) vision is "to align capital allocation and corporate behavior to wider goals of financial stability and sustainable development." It is focused on communicating short-, medium-, and long-term value. The IIRC identifies six capitals that need to be maintained to create value: financial, built or manufactured, natural, human, relationship or social, and intellectual. The IIRC is unique as it provides a sixth capital called intellectual. Most sources refer to five capitals. The idea behind integrated reporting is that all functional areas will integrate their thinking to achieve financial as well as sustainability goals through the maintenance of the capitals (Figure 2.2).

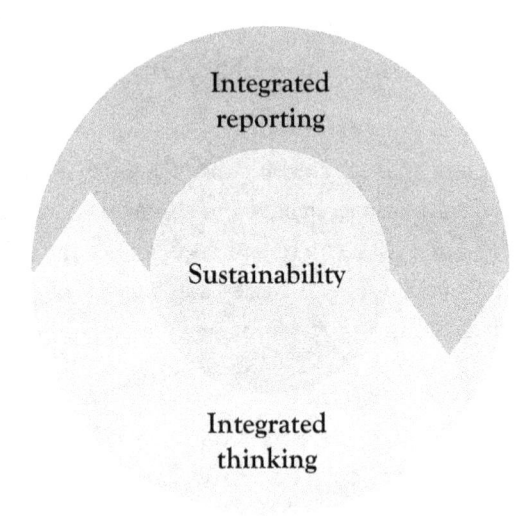

Figure 2.2 Integrated reporting = integrated thinking

Source: Based on IIRC, 2013

Reflection Integrated Reporting or Integrated Thinking: Which Comes First?

Background

The concept behind integrated reporting is that it brings the functional areas of a company together to develop integrated thinking about the role of each business function in the sustainability journey (e.g., accounting, marketing, law, production, customer service, finance, and others). In this way, the company places emphasis on value creation through maintenance of the capitals. Many companies have difficulty completing their first integrated report because they have little experience in integrated thinking.

Questions

Which do you think should come first: integrated reporting or integrated thinking? Will an attempt to produce an integrated report lead to integrated thinking or must a company first practice integrated thinking to be able to produce an integrated report?

SASB. In 2011 the Sustainability Accounting Standards Board (SASB) was established to develop industry-specific standards to disclose sustainability metrics in SEC-related filings in the United States. Rather than allowing the company to determine material topics (those most important to stakeholders and the company) as suggested under GRI Standards, SASB determines material topics for each industry and which indicators should be used. SASB focuses on sustainability issues that are the most financially important to investors. Table 2.2 compares characteristics of GRI and SASB.

Table 2.2 Comparison of GRI and SASB (based on GRI 2018; SASB 2019)

Characteristic	GRI	SASB
Target for use of standards	All reporting entities (profit and nonprofit, cities, etc.) worldwide.	Publicly held companies listed on exchanges in the United States but can be used by any company.
Process for determining risk and materiality	The entity level through stakeholder engagement.	The industry level by the SASB Standard Board.
Target for disclosures	All stakeholders.	Capital providers.

Unlike the GRI and the SASB which provide specific indicators and disclosures for sustainability reporting, IR instead provides a framework for bringing together all essential information necessary for decision making together in one report and does not suggest specific indicators (covered in Chapter 6).

Because climate change has become such an important concern regarding the resiliency of our planet and the financial risk associated with climate change to business operations, several organizations have suggested specific disclosures regarding climate. Three of the most well-known organizations are the CDP, the CDSB, and the TCFD.

CDP. In 2002 CDP (formerly known as the Carbon Disclosure Project) was formed to collect detailed information on carbon emissions by companies, cities, states, and regions. Carbon reporting is voluntary, but more than 7,000 companies and 620 cities worldwide provide information to the CDP, which is requested by investor institutions. It has now expanded to collecting disclosure on water and forests (CDP n.d.).

CDSB. In 2007 the Climate Disclosure Standards Board (CDSB) was formed as an international organization comprised of business and environmental NGOs that provide companies with a framework for environmental reporting. CDSB is working to adapt financial accounting standards to accounting for natural capital with its primary user as the investor (CDSB n.d.).

TCFD. In 2016 the Task Force on Climate-related Financial Disclosures (TCFD) was formed as an industry-led organization and recommends financial disclosures related to the climate that are useful for lenders, insurers, and investors with a strong focus on risk (TCFD n.d.).

Working Together: Corporate Reporting Dialogue

It is easy to feel overwhelmed by the number of policies, reporting guidelines/standards, climate-related disclosures, and the numerous other reporting requirements popping up from different organizations. If you feel overwhelmed, you can empathize with companies who try to satisfy all the requests for environmental and social information. The question then arises: Are these standard-setting organizations competing or cooperating? Are they separately creating standards that are duplicating efforts? Recently, these organizations started working together through the Corporate Reporting Dialogue. Table 2.3 compares the organizations on purpose, preparer, and user of the report.

Initially (1990s), a variety of secondary stakeholders pressured companies for accountability and were the loudest critics. At that time, most members of the financial community (financial institutions, financial analysts, stock markets, and investors) did not see sustainability reporting as useful or relevant to them. Part of the concern by the financial

Table 2.3 Corporate reporting dialogue participants

Organization	Primary Purpose	Primary Preparer of Report	Primary Users (stakeholders) of Report
International Organization for Standardization (ISO)	All types of standards but ISO 26000 covers sustainability	Not applicable. Addresses performance and not reporting	Not applicable. Addresses performance and not reporting
International Accounting Standards Board (IASB)	Financial reporting standards	Publicly held corporations worldwide	Providers of financial capital
Financial Accounting Standards Board (FASB) (observer)	Financial reporting standards	Publicly held corporations headquartered in the United States	Providers of financial capital
International Integrated Reporting Council (IIRC)	Sustainability reporting in an integrated financial report (value creation based on six capitals)	Publicly held corporations worldwide	Providers of financial capital
Global Reporting Initiative (GRI)	Sustainability reporting standards (based on economic, environmental, and social)	Any type of entity worldwide	All stakeholders (primary and secondary)
Sustainability Accounting Standards Board (SASB)	Sustainability reporting standards	Publicly held companies in the United States	Providers of financial capital
CDP (carbon, forestry, water)	Carbon, forest, and water reporting to own database	Publicly held companies worldwide	All stakeholders
Climate Disclosure Standards Board (CDSB)	Environmental disclosures in financial reports	Publicly held companies worldwide	Providers of financial capital

Note: The Task Force on Climate-related Financial Disclosures (TCFD) is not a member of Corporate Reporting Dialogue. Based on IIRC Corporate Reporting Dialogue 2019.

community was the credibility of the information and the lack of knowledge of how to use it. In the early 2000s, to provide more credibility to sustainability reports, companies were experimenting with assurance statements. As they improved their information systems and gained more experience in reporting, data became more accurate. However, verification is not widespread at this time (discussed in Chapter 7). (See Figure 2.3.)

As more evidence revealed that attention to sustainability is an important business concern and can affect financial progress both negatively and positively, the financial community has shown more interest. Now, many leading companies assess the risks and opportunities associated with satisfactory and unsatisfactory environmental and social performance to understand the relationship to financial performance, but there is still much to learn. As a result of the financial community's awareness of the relationship between environmental/social and financial performance, many financially related institutions are now setting standards for sustainability reporting as well.

Reflection: Sustainability Reporting for the Financial Community Versus All Stakeholders

GRI sets sustainability reporting standards considering all organizations, and all stakeholders are entitled to know an organization's sustainability process. Although sustainability reporting started out with a few pages in the annual financial report (mostly qualitative), later companies moved to stand-alone reports. Currently, once again, leading companies are integrating social and environment activities within the annual financial disclosure. More recently, sustainability disclosure is not a separate section in the report, but integrated with the financial disclosure, showing how sustainability complements their financial performance.

Now that the financial community has interest in sustainability disclosure and feels that it belongs along with annual financial disclosure, will the secondary stakeholders (such as communities, environmental NGOs, regulators, and others who do not normally read financial reports) be sidelined and their information needs be left unfulfilled?

THE CONCEPT OF SUSTAINABILITY REPORTING   35

Mid 2000
Reported financial social environmental performance in one integrated report

2000s
Used third-party verifications

Late 90s
Used reporting standards

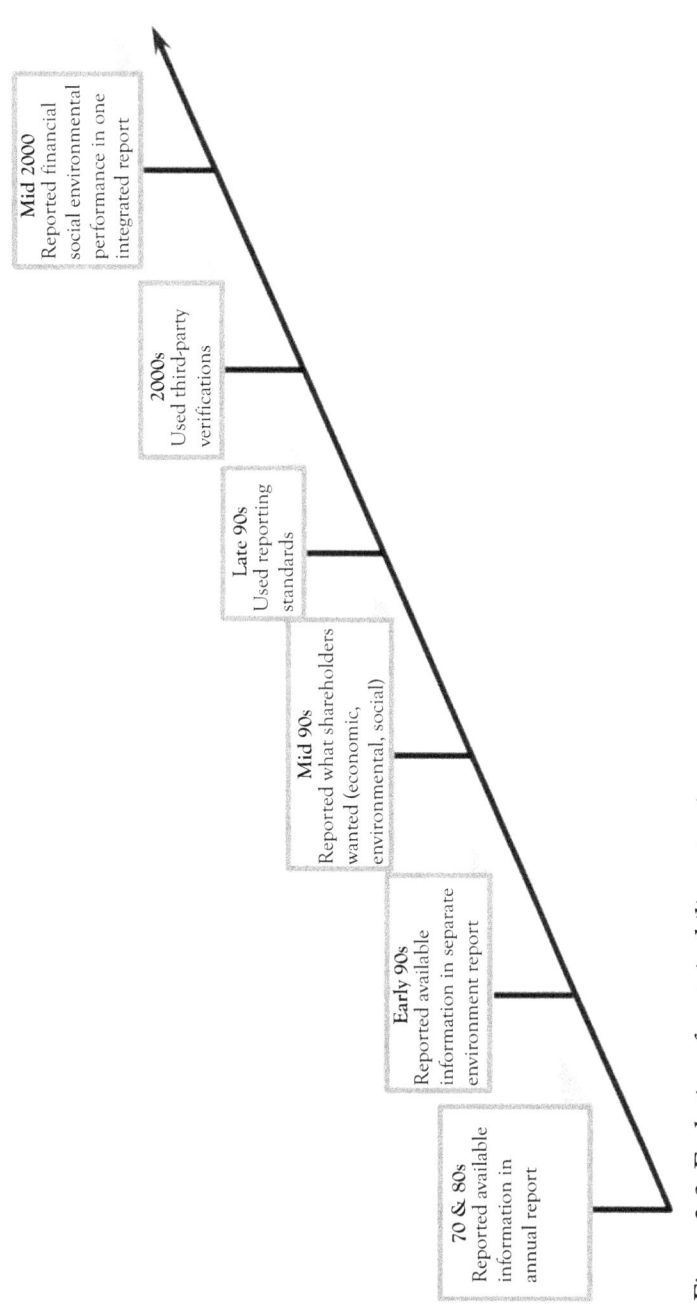

Mid 90s
Reported what shareholders wanted (economic, environmental, social)

Early 90s
Reported available information in separate environment report

70 & 80s
Reported available information in annual report

Figure 2.3 Evolution of sustainability reporting

Rater Organizations. In the early 1980s *Fortune* magazine provided the results of its annual survey of corporate reputation within an article in its magazine. One of the characteristics on which companies were rated by their peers was "responsibility to the community/environment." Subsequently, as investor interest in sustainability continued to increase, in 1999 in a separate initiative the Dow Jones Sustainability Index (DJSI) was launched through a partnership between the investment company SAM and the Dow Jones. The original DJSI included only the top 10 percent of companies in each sector based on their ratings on environmental, social, and governance (ESG) dimensions. To select companies for the Index, SAM provides a very detailed survey that companies complete if they wish to be considered for the Index. Cross-checking is done to ensure the answers to the survey are valid representations of the companies' activities (DJSI n.d.).

Reflection: Rating Agencies

The idea of a quick and easy rating system on the dimensions of sustainability is very attractive. However, the integrity of the rating depends on the credibility of the source of the data, the rigor and transparency of the methodology, the relevancy of the topics rated, and the experience of the rating team. Not all rating agencies offer equal quality. Some do not fully disclose their methodology as they consider it proprietary. Some of the rating organizations perceived as having the highest quality are listed below:

RobecoSam Corporate Sustainability Assessment

MSCI ESG Ratings

CDP Climate, Water & Forest Scores

Sustainalytics ESG Risk Ratings

Perform your own evaluation of these rating agencies and determine if you agree.

Source: SustainAbility (2019)

Investment firms especially want to know if there is a business case for sustainability but need a method to distinguish leaders from laggards. With sustainability demands on the rise, an entire rating industry has emerged. Rater organizations score companies on different aspects of their ESG (the governance dimension is substituted for the economic dimension). Sustainability reports are a major source of information to develop rating scores. Academic and professional research often investigates if companies following a sustainable path still provide an acceptable shareholder value or if there is a trade-off. In 2005, the United Nations worked with a group of institutional investors to develop the Principles of Responsible Investing (PRI) to align investor and societal objectives. Now asset managers, institutional investors, stock exchanges, and others are all interested in companies' ESG scores to attempt to follow PRI (PRI n.d.).

Key Takeaways

- Even though a company could have excellent sustainability performance, if the company does not report its performance, stakeholders will be hindered in their decision making, and the company misses an opportunity to learn about its own performance.
- When key events harm the financial community or new financial instruments/transactions are created, financial reporting standards are revised. Sustainability reporting is similar. Important sustainability disasters motivated change in performance and reporting.
- Two key events were the Bhopal gas leak and the Exxon Valdez oil spill. Both events spurred a change in performance through policies/guidelines and related reporting requirements on adherence to the policies/guidelines.
- The mid-2000s brought a proliferation of sustainability reporting guidelines. Some guidelines are broad based, covering all aspects of sustainability and all organizations. Other guidelines are on a specific aspect, such as carbon, forest, or water, or a specific industry, such as resource extractive.

- The GRI has provided the most well-known, broad-based set of sustainability reporting standards and sector guidelines used today for stand-alone reports. The Standards are complementary to IR, which suggests a framework for maintenance of the value-creating capitals.
- SASB has determined which indicators belong in financial reports filed with securities commissions and which are material for each sector.
- Other organizations, such as CDP, CDSB, and TCFD, have focused more narrowly on environmental aspects of sustainability.
- The Corporate Reporting Dialogue has brought standard-setting organizations together to ensure harmonization. A mapping tool on its website provides clarity on purpose, scope, and content of each of the participants in the Corporate Reporting Dialogue.
- Rater organizations have sprung up to fulfill a need to compare companies on sustainability. The integrity of the ratings relies on quality and transparency of methods and availability of information.

Corporate sustainability is a business approach that creates long-term shareholder value by embracing opportunities and managing risks . . . to harness the market's potential for sustainable products and services while at the same time successfully reducing and avoiding sustainability costs and risks.

—Dow Jones Sustainability Index

CHAPTER 3

Sustainability at the Organization Level

Main purpose: Comprehend how an organization begins a sustainability journey and the importance of engaging stakeholders throughout the journey.

Objectives: After reading this chapter, you should be able to do the following:

- Describe the major dimensions of a model that depicts a sustainable organization.
- Interrelate the linkage between the stakeholders' materiality assessment and an organization's policy, performance, and reporting to recognize and incorporate diverse values.
- Explain the different methods that organizations use to determine materiality of topics within the economic, social, and environmental dimensions of sustainability.
- Identify how stakeholders can provide guidance on the sustainability process.

Exceptional businesses sustain bottom-line results, which they invest to create meaningful, positive impact for their stakeholders.

—Punit Renjen

Now that we have a strong foundation in the basics of sustainability performance and reporting and how they have evolved over the last few decades, we will learn how an organization gets started on its sustainability journey. Although the emphasis in this book is on the sustainability of companies, the term "entity" or "organization" suggests that sustainability is a journey that everyone must take (all types of organizations and individuals). We all have a stake in, and a responsibility to care for, our little corner of the world. When possible, we should help others take care of their corners when they are unable to do so. In this matter, we all will experience a better quality of life. Ideally, through our value creation activities we should each leave this planet in a better condition than when we arrived.

Some organizations have registered concern about the lack of a clear detailed definition of sustainability, and therefore they delay their actions because of this. Agreed, a good map makes the journey easier, but if we never look beyond what we know and with what we are comfortable, we will never start learning. We need some organizations to be pioneers (to make the map). In this way, it will be easier for others to know the way. André Gide said it well in this quote: *You can never cross the ocean until you have the courage to lose sight of the shore.*

To learn something new often requires a little struggling and feeling of discomfort to get to a deeper level of understanding, but it brings increased awareness and knowledge. Therefore, organizations have had to struggle with what sustainability means to their own employees and their specific stakeholders. This struggling process has brought greater understanding of how to customize sustainability for relevancy.

Organizational Model for Sustainability and ASICS Example

As we have learned in Chapter 1, there are many overarching models that we could use to illustrate sustainability at a high level, but most entities need detail to implement sustainability at a company or organization level. The model used here for implementing sustainability for an organization depicts the interconnectedness among three main dimensions: (a) policies (beliefs and values), (b) performance (activities), and (c) stakeholders' needs and desires (based on the work of Zenisek 1979). In summary, the model illustrates that the sustainability journey starts with a policy (a plan) to guide the organization in its performance. However, this policy should be congruent with what its stakeholders need and desire. The policy also must be implemented through the organization's actions, resulting both in performance accomplishments and challenges.

```
        Policy          Management
                         systems              Performance
          ⟺                                        
                     ⟵⟶

    Participation                        Sustainability
   in multi-stakeholder                    reporting
       initiatives                        and assurance
              ⟶                    ⟵

                    Stakeholder needs
                      and desires
```

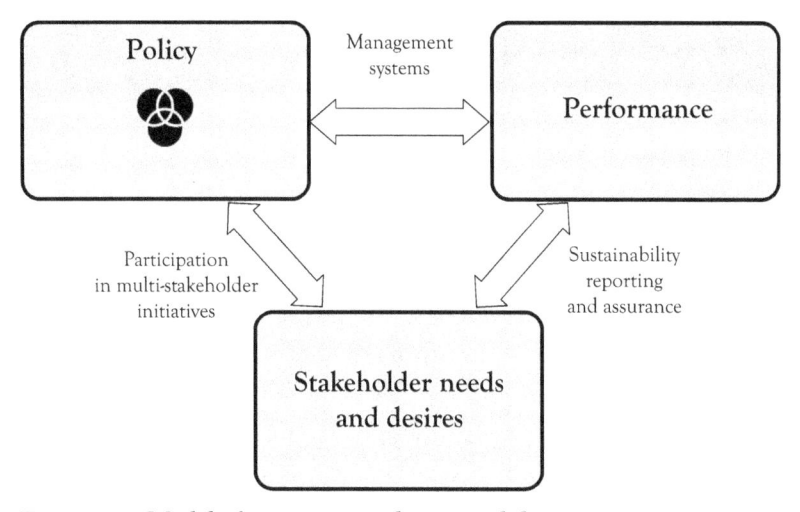

Figure 3.1 Model of organizational sustainability

Source: Based on Zenisek 1979

Finally, periodically the entity reports on its activities to determine if it is in line with the stakeholders' expectations. Subsequently, the stakeholders might recommend changes for certain aspects of the policy, performance, or both (Figure 3.1).

Notice that the arrows in the model go both ways, which suggests consistency and feedback among the dimensions. Consequently, the question arises as to how the organization maintains this consistency among the three dimensions.

A strong sustainability management system (SMS) links the policy with performance. Initially, an SMS was called an environmental management system (EMS) before social became more prominent. Participation in multi-stakeholder initiatives keeps the entity attuned to stakeholders' evolving needs and wants, and the many forms of sustainability reporting provide stakeholders with information about the entity's performance.

Each of the dimensions in this model and the links between the three dimensions deserve a more in-depth discussion. Alongside the explanation of each dimension, we see how ASICS, a global sporting apparel and shoe company, applies the model. (Figure 3.2) ASICS mission is "I Move Me" meaning the company's purpose is to help individuals create a sound body and a sound mind by producing products for "people who move and want to start moving." However, the movement starts with each individual or me. Furthermore, the "I Move Me" is expanded to "I Move Me Smarter" (pertaining to a healthier planet—the environment) and "I Move Me Stronger" (pertaining to supporting healthy workplaces, supply chains, and local communities—social). See ASICS report for more details about the examples used.

Policies and Stakeholders' Needs and Desires. Within the context that a company operates (e.g., country, sector, region, and business model), it must create a policy statement or several policy statements that describe the organization's values and planned activities on its sustainability journey. Stakeholders should influence every aspect of the company's sustainability process, from the material topics that are included in the policy, to evaluating and providing feedback on the organization's progress. Stakeholders will not all have the same needs and desires; therefore, it is important to identify stakeholder groups, analyze the topics that are similar/different among groups, and determine what actions are necessary to address their needs and desires. The policy should then be approved by the board of directors and implemented by everyone in the company through a set of objectives for each upcoming year.

ASICS Example. Even though ASICS has a range of guidelines and procedures, two major policies guide their sustainability journey: (a) ASICS Global Code of Conduct and (b) ASICS Global Policy on the Environment. (Figure 3.2) ASICS has identified 12 material issues (materiality matrix), stakeholder groups, and the company's primary activities and interactions with each. Two topics receiving priority are product safety/quality and ethical workplace standards. Each material topic is matched to its value chain analysis, from raw materials to end-of-life disposal.

Participation in Multi-stakeholder Initiatives. When we surround ourselves by like-minded people, which most of us do, we will probably start to believe that all others have the same beliefs and opinions that we do. Therefore, it is important to take the opportunity to participate in events and activities that will expose us to others' positions and points of view. These diverse beliefs and opinions are voiced through memberships in multi-stakeholder initiatives to help stay connected. Organizations with diverse opinions could be climate change institutions, regulatory agencies, industry associations, environmental groups, trade associations, and more.

SUSTAINABILITY AT THE ORGANIZATION LEVEL   43

```
┌─────────────────────────┐      • Board of directors
│ • Global code of conduct│      • Sustainability report    ┌─────────────────────────┐
│ • Global policy on      │      • ISO 14001                │ Progress on the 5-year  │
│   environment           │ ⇔                               │   strategic growth plan │
│ • Others                │                                 │                         │
└─────────────────────────┘                                 └─────────────────────────┘
              • AFIRM                                  • GRI Sustainability report
              • ILO Better work                        • CDP
              • SAC                                    • Sustainable development goals
              • Others                                 • Integrated reporting in the future
                        ┌───────────────────────────────┐
                        │ Materiality issues incorporated│
                        │ into the value change analysis │
                        │    (product life cycle)        │
                        └───────────────────────────────┘
```

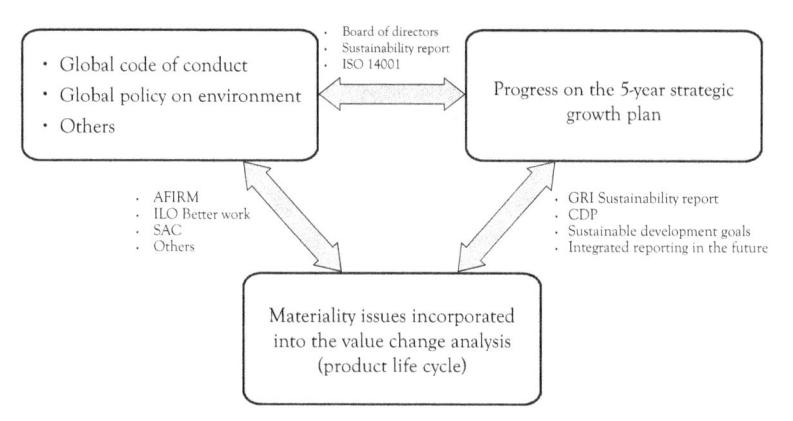

Figure 3.2 ASICS: model of organizational sustainability. I Move Me: Smarter, Stronger

(Note: The model was assembled from discussions in various parts of ASICS' "I Move Me" Sustainability Report, 2017)

ASICS Example. ASICS participates in a number of initiatives. Three are mentioned here: (a) Apparel and Footwear International RSL (Restricted Substances List) Management Group (AFIRM), (b) International Labor Organization (ILO) Better Work, and (c) Sustainable Apparel Coalition (SAC) (Figure 3.2).

Management System. The organization must set up a management system (EMS or SMS) which acts as a form of control system to ensure that the objectives set out in the policy are reached. This system should ensure that the risks associated with accomplishing the objectives are identified and mitigated. Impact assessments, life cycle analyses, environmental and social costing, eco-design, environmental audits, ecological footprint calculations, and environmental liability estimates are tools that are part of the management system.

ASICS Example. ASICS's management system has ultimate responsibility resting with the Board of Directors through a Sustainability Department. It is in the process of establishing ISO 14001 environmental management systems at all of its locations worldwide. It regularly performs internal, commissioned, and partner audits throughout the year (Figure 3.2).

Performance. A set of indicators measure progress in achieving the objectives. The indicators evolve from key words and phrases in the policy statements. Feedback should be encouraged to monitor progress with internal stakeholders.

ASICS Example. A five-year strategic plan (based on its mission and material topics matrix) guides performance. Objectives and targets are set for the upcoming year and into the future. Progress is reported for six key areas and their subcategories (Figure 3.2).

Sustainability Reporting. Although the stand-alone sustainability report is the most common form for providing performance to its stakeholders, other forms of reporting such as websites, annual reports, carbon emissions reporting, safety reports, and more are also used. Feedback should be encouraged from external stakeholders as well.

ASICS Example. In addition to using GRI Standards to prepare its "I Move Me" Sustainability Report, ASICS also reports its carbon emissions performance to CDP. The company has identified Sustainability Development Goals (SDGs) 3, 6, 8, 12, and 13 as those that specifically apply to the company. It is working toward integrated reporting for the future. Deloitte Tohmatsu Sustainability Company provides assurance for the report (Figure 3.2).

Setting Policies Based on Stakeholders' Needs and Desires

We all value things differently. Generally, diversity is considered as a precious resource unless we are so intolerant of another's view that we will not recognize it as valid. Diversity of opinion helps us to question our own thinking and determine if our point of view could be improved. Organizations also have diverse values, which means they place different emphasis on the three sustainability dimensions (economic, social, and environment) or certain aspects within the three sustainability dimensions. Even though the economic dimension is essential to support the environment and social dimensions, companies might be overly concerned to please their shareholders with high returns on their stock investments to the detriment of the communities that buy their products, which eventually will harm their revenue flows. This lack of recognition of the stakeholders affected by a company's operating practices could be disastrous in the long term. Therefore, this section covers the highlighted dimensions of Figure 3.3.

SUSTAINABILITY AT THE ORGANIZATION LEVEL   45

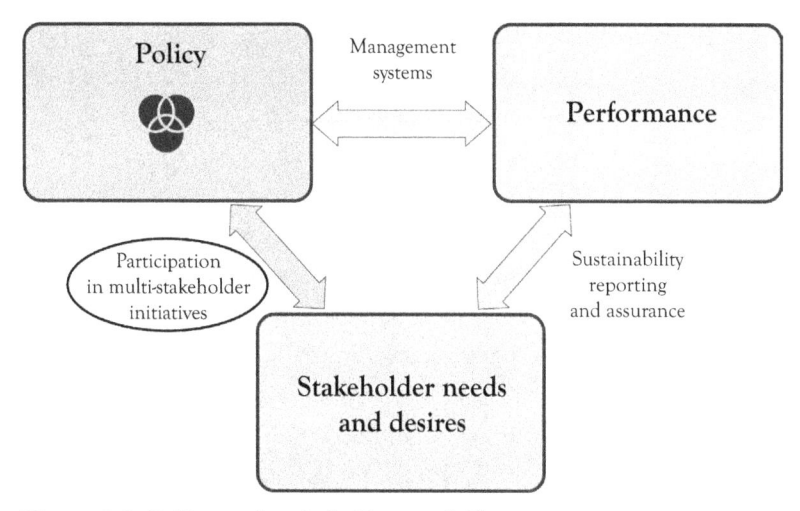

Figure 3.3 Policy and stakeholder needs/desires

Source: Based on Zenisek 1979

Many values are important on a sustainability journey. For illustration purposes, we use three values to understand why stakeholder engagement (asking stakeholders what is important) is an essential passenger to guide companies on their journeys. Each of these three values is illustrated on a continuum in Figure 3.4: (a) short-term versus long-term thinking, (b) self- versus community interest, and (c) priority of humans versus equality of all nature (Kluckhorn and Strodtbeck 1961; Milne 1996).

Organizations whose values lean more toward long-term planning, community interest, and equal treatment of humans and other forms of nature tend to set higher expectations for sustainability. Why?

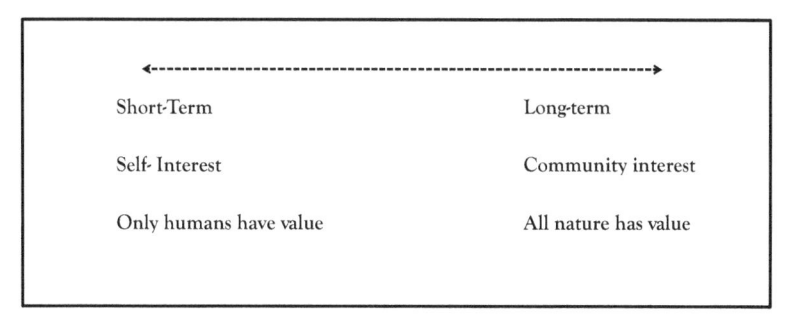

Short-Term	Long-term
Self- Interest	Community interest
Only humans have value	All nature has value

Figure 3.4 Values orientation

Source: Based on the work of Milne 1996; Kluckhorn and Strodbeck 1961

- Short-term versus Long-term Thinking: Long-term projects that integrate environmental and social might take longer to reap an economic return and the impact is harder to measure. Long-term thinking conserves resources for future generations rather than the current generation alone.
- Self- versus Community Interest: Resources, such as air, land, and waterways, even though they are not owned by individuals, need an authority such as the government to take care of them. As well, even if resources are owned by individuals or corporations, community interest should motivate conservative use thereby ensuring sufficient resources for future generations.
- Priority of Humans versus Nature: Using an example of our forests, some feel that all resources are useful only for products that humans can enjoy, such as trees for lumber and paper. Others think of trees as a shelter on a warm day, a place to find escape, a source of beauty and spirituality especially in the fall when leaves change color. A tree is also valuable just as a tree and not necessarily for the products it can provide for humans.

Given these different points of view of groups of stakeholders, it is important to incorporate these views within an organization's policies to guide its sustainability journey.

Reflection: Your Value Set

Where do you think you sit on each of the value scales? Think about activities in which you have engaged that would suggest you tend to be a long-term or short-term thinker, self- versus community-oriented, or how you prioritize the value of humans versus nature. Think of an event that happened recently in your life that would help you understand your position on the scales.

Off-the-shelf versus Customized Policies. There are off-the-shelf or universal policies that can be used by an organization, such as the UN Global Compact (10 principles that cover human rights, labor, environment, and anticorruption) or the OECD Guidelines for Multinational Enterprises (discussed in Chapter 2). These policies are created by global multi-stakeholder groups; therefore, they already reflect the views of diverse stakeholders. However, they usually contain very high-level statements that must be interpreted in the operating context of the organization and may not reflect the very specific concerns of local stakeholders.

An organization must ask the question: How do each of these policies apply to my specific circumstances? Different sectors and industries have different priorities regarding the dimensions of sustainability. Here are a few examples. An energy company has concerns about the reduction of greenhouse gas emissions, which could be causing climate change. A mining company or a cell phone manufacturer might prioritize human rights if they are using conflict minerals (minerals that originate from areas in which there is armed violence or instability). For example, cobalt is a conflict mineral used for making lithium-ion batteries, and it is highly likely that these are used in electronic devices. A textile firm might direct its attention to the "fast fashion trend" of throwaway clothes and develop systems that can ensure clothing does not end up in the land fill. A running shoe manufacturer could prioritize working conditions, especially in developing countries, where its factories are situated.

A customized policy with input from stakeholders provides additional confidence that the organization has included aspects of importance (material aspects). Eventually when the company is ready to report on its performance, the dimensions of reporting should be consistent with the policy dimensions. Otherwise, readers might assume that the company is not reporting on a topic because it is trying to hide its bad performance. Even though organizations might assume they know exactly what their stakeholders expect, a dialogue between a company and one of its stakeholders illustrates why stakeholder engagement is necessary.

Sustainability in Action: Why Engage Stakeholders?

Forestry Company: I think we have an excellent record of maintaining a sustainable stock of forests through our replanting program.

Environmental Scientist: I would agree your record is quite good; however, what we really want to know about is your performance on biodiversity.

Forestry Company: Biodiversity? How do we come up with indicators to monitor and report on biodiversity? That is quite difficult to do.

Environmental Scientist: Well, I am not sure at this time, but perhaps we could work together to find a way to report on this critical issue.

Material Topics: Many organizations offer excellent advice on stakeholder engagements. For our purposes, we will discuss two pioneers in the field and the advice that they offer.

- AccountAbility, a global consulting and standards firm.
- Global Reporting Initiative, a sustainability reporting standards setting organization.

Note that both of these organizations recognize stakeholder engagement as a continuous process that operates in tandem with the company as it takes on its sustainability journey.

AccountAbility's AA1000SES definition of stakeholder engagement emphasizes the accountability principles of inclusivity, materiality, and responsiveness:

Stakeholder engagement is the process used by an organization to engage relevant stakeholders for a clear purpose to achieve agreed outcomes. (AccountAbility 2015, p. 5)

To fulfill GRI's reporting principle of stakeholder inclusiveness, GRI requires that the "reasonable expectations and interest of stakeholders are considered" through a process that is systematic and should result in ongoing learning and strengthening trust (GRI 2018, p. 8). GRI provides extensive advice on stakeholder engagement to identify which topics are material to stakeholders. However, in brief, organizations take three steps suggested by GRI that describe the process of learning from stakeholders:

- Identify issues and create a list of topics;
- Prioritize what is material to the organization and recognize any potential conflicts or different perspectives through a form of stakeholder panel;

- Review the topics by an internal, high-level committee/team or an external consultant.

Similar to meeting financial objectives, environmental and social objectives have various risks and rewards associated with them. Management and stakeholders should discuss the benefits and difficulties that they could incur in achieving the objectives and the associated targets that come out of the objectives. Organizations use various sources to create a list of topics, such as news, social media, peer companies' reports, and industry trends. To prioritize the material topics in the list, organizations should send out a survey, have a telephone conversation, or hold an in-person stakeholder group meeting to rate and discuss the topics on two dimensions: (a) impact to the organization and (b) significance to the shareholders. This process generally results in what is called a materiality matrix, often provided in the sustainability report. These topics then form the basis for management to develop policies, to determine yearly objectives and their implementation, and to report to their stakeholders on their progress through the year-end sustainability report. The results of Samsung's Engagement, based on GRI, are illustrated in Table 3.1. The process distinguishes between different types of stakeholders, their concerns, communication lines with each set of stakeholders, and the strategy to address the concerns.

Table 3.1 Samsung and stakeholder engagement

STAKEHOLDER	KEY CONCERNS OF STAKEHOLDERS	COMMUNICATION CHANNEL
Suppliers	• Fair trade • Shared growth • Employees' human rights protection • Supplier's assessment for their impacts on society	• Hotline, Cyber Shinmungo, etc. • Supplier meetings, Win-Win Cooperation Day, etc. • Shared Growth Academy • Management counseling group for supplier
NGOs, CSR Councils, Specialized Institutions	• Social responsibility for local communities and the environment • Contribution to the UN SDGs • Transparent and prompt information disclosure	• Business networking events • Open and transparent engagement with NGOs

Governments	• Indirect economic effects • Fair trade • Health and safety • Compliance	• Attend policy debates • Attend council meetings • Participate in policy consultative bodies
Local Communities	• Local recruitment, local economy revitalization, and other indirect economic effects • Local environmental protection • Donation, volunteering, and other social giving initiatives	• Local volunteer centers • Local community council • Samsung Nanum Village • Local Community Blog (Suwon, Gumi, and Gwangju sites) • Yongin Hwaseong community Blog (http://www.sotongsamsung.com)
Customers	• Product/service quality • Safe product use • Correct product information • Transparent communication	• Customer satisfaction surveys conducted by external organizations • Call centers, service centers • Prosumer programs • Samsung Electronics Newsroom • Samsung Semicon Story • Young Samsung Community
Shareholders & Investors	• Economic outcomes • Risk management • Information sharing • Environmental, Social and Governance factors	• Investor Relations meetings • General shareholder meetings • One-on-one meetings • Analyst Day • Samsung Electronics' Corporate Firms YouTube URL: https://www.youtube.com/samsungelectronics
Employees	• Workplace health and safety • Diversity and equal opportunity • Training and career development • Employment and benefits • Labor relations	• Work Council • Counseling centers • Satisfaction surveys • Samsung LiVE • Newsletters • Reporting systems(compliance, ethics)

Source: Samsung Electronics 2018

The Materiality Matrix, derived from the stakeholder engagement process, becomes the foundation on which the sustainability report is prepared. For example in Figure 3.5, on the vertical axis of Teck's matrix "Influence on Assessment and Decisions on Communities of Interest"

SUSTAINABILITY AT THE ORGANIZATION LEVEL   51

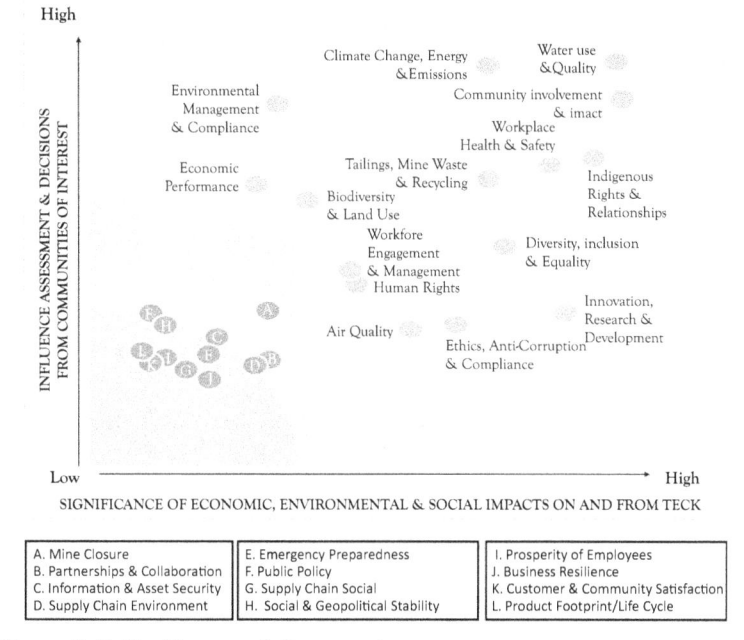

Figure 3.5 Teck's materiality matrix

Source: Teck 2017

essentially means the importance of these topics to stakeholders and runs from low to high. On the horizontal axis "Significance of Economic, Environmental and Social Aspects on and from Teck" means the impact of the company, again running from low to high. Those topics rating high on both axes (top right) are the topics that Teck should definitely address in its performance and its reporting. Management might not include other topics in the sustainability report but could provide information on the website or address them in some other appropriate matter.

Companies can engage with stakeholders through a number of different approaches depending on the significance and impact of the topic and the specific characteristics and expectations of the stakeholder group. To keep informed, many stakeholders will be satisfied with periodic communication coming from the company. Some will want more direct responses from management on specific issues. Yet, others might join forces with the company to work together on initiatives, thus involving the stakeholder as a change agent. Table 3.1 and Figure 3.6 provide additional information on these approaches.

Table 3.2 Types of stakeholder engagement

Informing: strong one-way communication (from firm to the stakeholders)	Responding: strong one-way, weak return communication (strong from firm to stakeholder; weak from stakeholder to firm)	Involving: strong two-way communication (from firm to stakeholder and from stakeholder to firm)
Newsletters	Consultation on material items or appropriateness of reports	Project monitoring
Regional or global sustainability reports on all dimensions	Grievance management; answering questions about certain aspects of a project	Negotiations
Reports on specific concerns or commitments	Informal sessions or town meeting on project process	Partnerships

Based on the work of Bowen et al. (2010) and Morsing and Schultz (2006)

Even though not all stakeholder groups or advisory panels will participate in every stakeholder engagement activity (Figure 3.6), stakeholders might help the company with the following:

- identifying material sustainability concerns and issues,
- determining the communication strategy appropriate for each stakeholder group,
- assessing performance on material topics,
- determining the credibility of the sustainability disclosure and report,
- deciding which company decisions need to be explained, and
- participating in projects with certain stakeholders to improve performance.

SUSTAINABILITY AT THE ORGANIZATION LEVEL   53

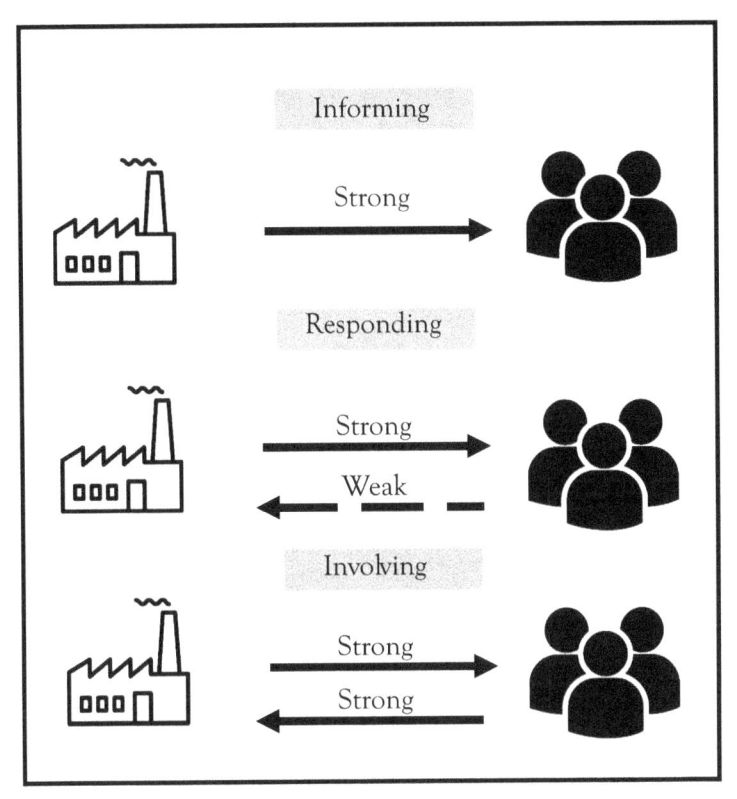

Figure 3.6 Types of stakeholder engagement

Source: Based on Bowen at 2000; Morsing and Schultz 2006.

Engaging with stakeholders might help prevent shareholder resolutions at a company's annual general meeting by identifying and addressing important issues early. Here is an example of a shareholder proposal that appeared in McDonald's proxy statement.

Sustainability in Action: Shareholder Proposals

RESOLVED: Shareholders request that McDonald's Corporation ("McDonald's") issue a report to shareholders, to be prepared at reasonable cost and omitting confidential and proprietary information, regarding the business risks associated with its continued use of plastic straws, and the company's efforts to develop and implement substitutes for plastic straws in its restaurants.

Source: McDonald's Corporation (2018; pp. 72–73) (see the document for McDonald's answer)

Check your favorite company's proxy statement to see if any proposals were presented on social or environmental concerns for shareholder vote.

Key Takeaways

- A sustainable company will link its policy (plan) to what it actually does (performance), and both will be consistent with stakeholder needs and desires.
- Strong management systems connect the policy and performance. Participation in multi-stakeholder initiatives connects the policy to stakeholders' needs and desires. Sustainability reporting connects performance to stakeholders' needs and desires.
- Stakeholders often differ in their values regarding short-term versus long-term thinking, self-interest versus community interest, and the value placed on humans versus other forms of life.
- Many off-the-shelf or universal policies, such as the Global Compact, give organizations good direction for their sustainability journey; however, most of these policies provide overarching principles that should be customized to the organization's specific stakeholder needs.
- Engaging with stakeholders will give companies direction on which specific topics of sustainability should be emphasized in specific locations or with specific stakeholder groups.

- Companies engage stakeholders in a number of different ways. Companies following GRI Sustainability Reporting Standards engage stakeholders to determine which topics they feel are significant to them and have the greatest impact on the company. These topics are frequently reviewed by internal managers as well.
- GRI Standards require companies to work with their stakeholders to complete the following steps: identify topics, prioritize them with stakeholders, and review them by internal managers and employees.
- Priority topics are then plotted in a matrix which is often found in the sustainability report. These matrices guide companies' performance and reporting priorities.
- Depending on the activity, companies might inform, respond to, or involve stakeholders through their engagement processes.

Stakeholder engagement is essential for answering the question: Is our policy still valid in a changing business context? As well as reporting on our policy, we need to challenge our policy, our objectives, our targets, all of that, to determine if they are in the right place.

—Anonymous Reporting Company

CHAPTER 4

Management Systems for Sustainability

Main purpose: Comprehend the role of management systems to link the policy with performance.

Objectives: After reading this chapter, you should be able to do the following:

- Describe major parts of a model for organizational sustainability with the policy and objectives as inputs and performance as the output, eventually leading to the sustainability report.
- Assess governance structure for ensuring actions on sustainability.
- Identify procedures and approaches to instill commitment and develop capability.
- Distinguish between systems that motivate compliance versus innovation.

Sustainability is ingrained in every action we take across our business.

—Andrew Mackenzie, BHP CEO 2018, p. 3

A Systems Approach

To move from the policy to actual performance requires management systems to ensure that all the employees and contractors of the organization are moving in the same direction (Figure 4.1 illustrates the role of the systems). Once a strategy is formulated to implement the policy, systems (with many parts working together) are essential to fulfill the objectives and to meet targets. Often planning occurs at the top levels of management, but employees at all levels are part of the system, especially those

58 SUSTAINABILITY PERFORMANCE AND REPORTING

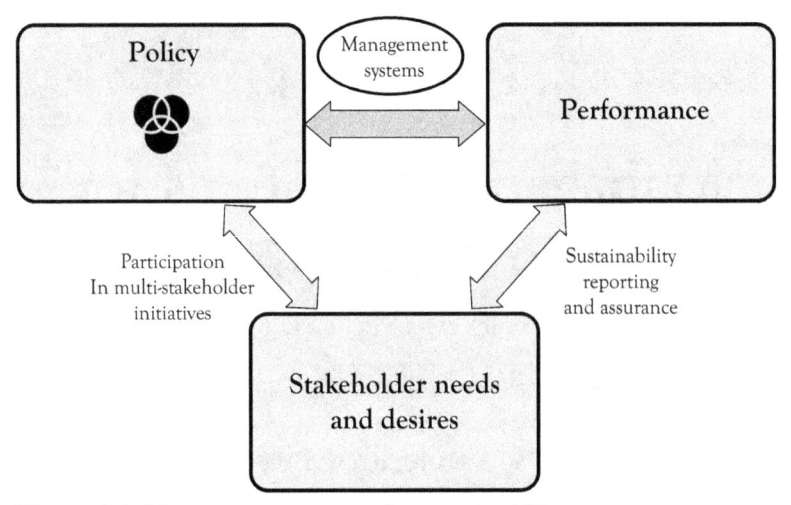

Figure 4.1 Management systems for sustainability

Source: Based on Zenisek 1979

out in the field or working at the operational level of the organization, who ultimately determine if the policy is carried out properly.

A system has many components or parts that work together to accomplish some outcome. These components might consist of structures, schemes, procedures, techniques, and methods that interact in harmony to achieve results. Regulations and laws also affect the development of a system. Regarding sustainability, we have economic systems, environmental/ecological systems, and social systems. The idea of sustainability is that these three systems will be synchronized to work together to accomplish objectives that are congruent. BHP, a global resources company, illustrates its system components and how they work together (BHP 2018) (Figure 4.2).

Standards for Sustainability Management Systems

The International Organization for Standardization, commonly called International Standards Organization (ISO), develops standards used worldwide to provide consistency in products, services, and processes between countries and regions. ISO uses a multi-stakeholder approach by including many countries and organizations in the process. Likely, the ISO 14000 series of standards are the most widely used for environmental management systems (EMS) and related tools to help organizations in their

Keeping ourselves accountable

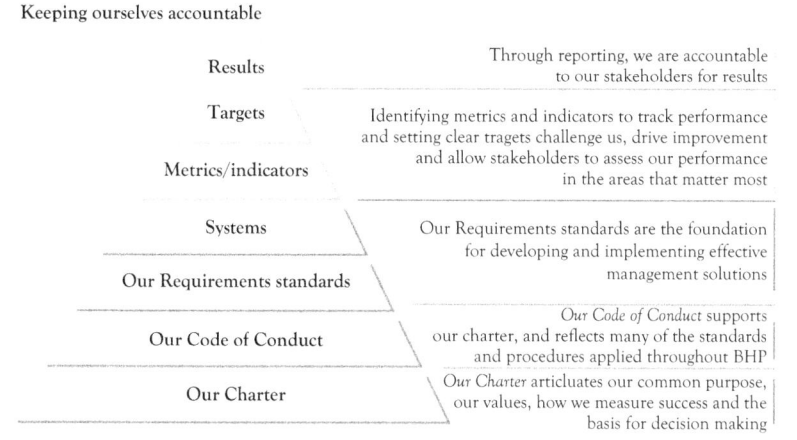

Results	Through reporting, we are accountable to our stakeholders for results
Targets	Identifying metrics and indicators to track performance and setting clear tragets challenge us, drive improvement and allow stakeholders to assess our performance in the areas that matter most
Metrics/indicators	
Systems	Our Requirements standards are the foundation for developing and implementing effective management solutions
Our Requirements standards	
Our Code of Conduct	Our Code of Conduct supports our charter, and reflects many of the standards and procedures applied throughout BHP
Our Charter	Our Charter articluates our common purpose, our values, how we measure success and the basis for decision making

Figure 4.2 BHP's managing sustainability

Source: BHP 2018

decision making. ISO14001 defines an EMS as part of an overall management system that includes the organizational structure, planning activities, responsibilities, practices, procedures, processes, developing resources, and implementing, achieving, reviewing, and maintaining the environmental policy (ISO 14001, 2015). ISO 26000 provides guidance on the social responsibility of all organizations and covers both environmental and social aspects. Table 4.1 lists a few of the many ISO standards and other standards that are helpful to develop sustainability management systems.

Table 4.1 Guidelines/standards for management systems

Standard	Title
ISO 14001	Environmental management systems—Requirements with guidance for use
ISO 14004	Environmental management systems—General guidelines on implementation
ISO 14006	Environmental management systems—Guidelines for incorporating eco-design
ISO 14040	Environmental management systems—Life cycle assessment—Principles and framework
ISO 14044	Environmental management systems—Life cycle assessment—Requirements and guidelines
ISO 14063	Environmental management—Environmental communication—Guidelines and examples
ISO 14064	Greenhouse case emissions

ISO 14065	Greenhouse gas emissions—Requirements for greenhouse gas validation and verification bodies for use in accreditation for other forms of recognition
ISO 26000	Guidance on social responsibility
OHSAS 18001	Standards for occupational safety and health management systems
SA 8000	Social certification standard for fair treatment of workers

Formal and Informal Systems

We might think of most of the components of management systems as formal systems that are effective in reducing uncertainty in employees' behavior. However, these components of the formal systems will be ineffective if the informal system does not support them. Components of the informal system, sometimes referred to as corporate culture, consist of shared values, beliefs, cultural traditions, trust, ethical climate, passion, motivation, and leadership, to name a few. Even though formal systems are necessary, a company will be more successful in achieving its objectives if the formal and informal systems are in harmony. If employees do not believe that a certain sustainability objective is important, it likely will not be accomplished (Figure 4.3).

Formal	Informal
• Organizational structure	• Values
• Planning activities	• Beliefs
• Responsibilities	• Cultural traditions
• Practices	• Trust
• Procedures	• Ethical climate
• Processes	• Leadership
• Training	• Passion
• Reviewing	• Motivation

Figure 4.3 System components: formal and informal

Management System Components: Commitment and Capability

Even though management systems comprise many components, we will discuss two overarching components that are essential for reaching sustainability objectives and fulfilling the company's policy. These two components are commitment and capability. Commitment and capability must run up and down all levels of the organization. Not only does an organization need strong motivation at the highest level of governance, but it also needs committed and capable employees throughout the various levels of management (COSO 2018; CICA n.d.) (Figure 4.4).

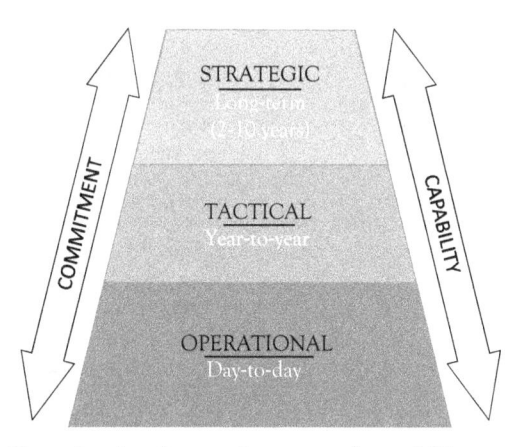

Figure 4.4 Organizational commitment and capability

For example, top management might create a waste diversion policy, which the board of directors approved (strategic commitment and capability). Consequently, the mid- to low-level managers create a plan for carrying out the policy (tactical commitment). They will need a budget for waste bins to separate waste and a method to communicate the plan to employees (tactical capability). They might also create a plan for incentives or rewards to recognize outstanding waste diverters (tactical commitment). In the field and in the office employees need to be aware of which items can be recycled to be able to sort the garbage into the proper waste bins (operational capability). Furthermore, the maintenance people must be motivated to ensure that the recyclable waste goes in the proper container for pick up (operational commitment). Without employees' commitments and capabilities to carry through on the recycling process at all levels, targets might not be accomplished. To ensure commitment and develop capability, managers and supervisors should integrate responsibility and accountability for various aspects of the sustainability policy/plan into the job duties of subordinates. Providing budget support and training is essential. Rewarding employees on their sustainability accomplishments also develops commitment. For a summary of these concepts, see Table 4.2.

Table 4.2 Commitment and capability at all organizational levels

Organizational Level	How Long Is the Involvement?	Who Is Involved?	How Are They Involved?
Strategic	Long-term plan (2–10 years)	Board of directors and top management team	Develop a vision, mission, strategy, and long-term objectives
Tactical	Short term (1-year goals and objectives)	Mid- and low-level managers and supervisor	Create a plan for each year, assigning responsibility, preparing a budget, hiring personnel, and providing incentives
Operational	Day-to-day activities (today, tomorrow, and month after month)	Employees in offices and in the field	Carry out the plan and monitor on a daily basis

Commitment

At the strategic level, the appropriate structure and composition of the board can create conduits for assimilation of different viewpoints. Some organizations have a separate committee of the board to ensure that sustainability issues get sufficient emphasis and to show commitment at the highest levels of the company. As the board members are instrumental in setting the strategic direction, they should reflect diverse experiences, genders, points of view, and channels for information flow to prevent myopic thought. The commitment and capabilities of the board members determine if the organization's definition of sustainability will be broad or narrow. At the highest level, the board members will monitor if the company's sustainable direction as expressed in its policy is reflected in corporate actions. Some organizations want to lead their sectors in the sustainability movement. Others just want to ensure that they are complying with all the laws and not incurring exceedances or infractions. Those decisions are made at the board level.

With strong "tone at the top," through a special board committee, the likelihood of accomplishing the objectives is greater. These committees carry various names, such as Public Affairs, Corporate Citizenship, and Environment, Health, and Safety. Other companies prefer to have a leadership committee with members from the top management team. Some have committees at both levels. As top management has to ensure implementation, responsibility lies with them. A leadership committee might consist of the Chief Executive Officer (CEO), various chief officers, various vice presidents, and a vice president in charge of sustainability. Wells Fargo's committee is at the board level and is titled Corporate Responsibility Committee. Nike has two committees: one at the board level and one at the top management team level.

Sustainability in Action: Board and Management Level Committees

Wells Fargo & Company's board level **Corporate Responsibility Committee** comprises four members who carry out the following responsibilities (edited):

- *oversee the Company's policies, programs, and strategies, including community development and reinvestment activities and performance, fair and responsible lending, government relations, support of charitable organizations, and environmental issues;*

- *monitor the Company's relationships with external stakeholders and the Company's reputation with its stakeholders;*

- *advise the Board of Directors and management on strategies that affect and enhance the Company's role and reputation among its stakeholders.*

Source: Wells Fargo & Company (2019, 68, 69)

Nike, Inc. also has a board committee titled **Corporate Responsibility and Sustainability Committee** with responsibilities similar to Wells Fargo's. **Nike** also has a **Performance and Disclosure Committee** at the top management level that "meets regularly to review sustainability targets, performance, and disclosures." It includes the following members:
- Chief Administrative Officer & General Counsel
- Chief Communications Officer
- Chief Financial Officer
- Chief Operating Officer
- Chief Sustainability Officer & VP Innovation Accelerator

Source: Nike (2016/2017, p. 5)

Once a strategic direction is determined through multi-stakeholder input, the tactical and operational systems must have sufficient structure and detail to ensure that they are functioning suitably to motivate employees to implement the strategic direction. These systems inform decision making that capitalizes on opportunities, aids in resource allocation, provides direction on sustainability initiatives, and monitors progress. Organizations can support commitment with these activities:

- Communicating the intended objectives throughout the organization to all levels of management and operations via newsletters, meetings, blogs, retreats, and other means.
- Assigning responsibility by having employees within various levels of management and operations who will champion and are responsible for fulfilling various objectives.
- Rewarding employees throughout the organization with awards, compensation, or both.

Sustainability in Action: Creating Commitment in Microsoft and Intel

Microsoft uses a carbon fee to internalize the cost of carbon created externally through the use of energy, such as business travel. The business group that consumes the related energy is charged the carbon fee as a budgeted and actual income statement line item. If the manager wants to show higher profits, one option is to reduce the carbon consumption for the business group.

Source: DiCaprio (2013).

Intel links employee compensation to the annual bonus.

Since 2008, we have linked a portion of our executive and employee compensation to corporate responsibility factors in our Annual Performance Bonus (APB). In 2017, the operational goals component included metrics related to our diversity and inclusion objectives. Previous metrics have focused on areas such as carbon emissions and recycling.

Source: Intel (2017–2018, p. 12). (See 2018 Proxy Statement for more information)

Capability

Capability to implement sustainability actions can be developed through a number of ways. Just as with commitment, capability must exist not only at the highest levels of the board and management but also at every level of the organization: strategic, tactical, and operational. Capability includes having the knowledge and expertise to carry out sustainability objectives. Capabilities can be developed in training sessions, seminars, workshops, conferences, and formal education, both in-house and external. Organizations can also hire capable people to fill internal gaps in expertise. Creating communities of learning (both internal and external) can help transfer information across organizations and bring new expertise to an organization. Working with suppliers and customers helps to address sustainability concerns or issues. In addition to having the knowledge and expertise, it is also important to provide adequate investments and operating budgets to ensure sustainability objectives can be accomplished. In summary, capability is supported by these activities:

- Allocating resources through budgets and investments;
- Hiring people with the required expertise;
- Building expertise internally through training; and
- Providing opportunities to learn from others internally and externally.

Good management systems supported by committed and capable employees will also ensure better compliance with regulations, thus preventing infractions rather than paying the associated fines, penalties, and clean-up costs. Expensive court costs and legal fees also take precious time away from mainstream business activities. Intel, a technology company, provides several examples in its sustainability report of how it develops capabilities in its workers.

Sustainability in Action: Capability at Intel

Training: *Each year, our CEO communicates with all employees and senior managers about the importance of ethics and legal compliance. This "tone from the top"—combined with our annual ethics and compliance training, regular communications throughout the year, and educational resources on our employee intranet site—help to create an ethical and legally compliant culture.*

Communities of Learning: *We have invested significant time and resources in collaborating with others to influence system-level, industry-wide improvements to protect and empower workers in the global* electronics supply chain and reduce community impacts. For more information, see the Supply Chain Responsibility section of this report.

Budget/Investment: *Reducing our energy use is a key component of our overall climate change strategy, and we have proactively invested in renewable energy purchasing and alternative energy installations.*

Source: Intel (2017–2018, p. 13, 15, 27)

Comply Versus Innovate

Most of our discussion thus far has been regarding commitment and capability to get employees and suppliers to comply with the company's policies to achieve sustainability objectives, such as complying with the waste diversion policy. However, another aspect of management systems that is critical for continuous improvement is to motivate employees to think critically about the systems that are currently operating and whether they could be improved. Employees can also innovate ways that sustainability might open opportunities for cost savings or new products that satisfy a changing demand. Employees can bring fresh ideas about improving the systems, such as innovative ways to avoid creating waste in the first place. Companies have systems that will motivate both compliance and innovation.

Sustainability in Action: Compliance and Innovate Systems at Johnson Matthey

Comply

Failure to comply with ethical and regulatory compliance standards leading to reputational damage, to civil or criminal legal exposure for the company or for individuals or to risk of contractual breach.

To mitigate the risk the company uses a code of ethics, tone from senior leaders, subject matter experts, legal compliance policies and procedures, a hotline, and an Ethics Panel.

> **Innovate**
>
> *Innovation is realising value from knowledge . . . We do not innovate in isolation and it's our strength of understanding across the value chain that accelerates our progress.*
>
> *To motivate innovation, the company identifies customer needs (economic, environmental, or social) and the value of that need, works with universities worldwide, sponsors PhDs, and combines core capabilities in science and technology with smart manufacturing.*
>
> Source: Johnson Matthey (2018, p. 80, 28)

It is easy for an organization to say that it is innovating for sustainability. However, it will not happen unless a management system is designed to motivate creative and innovative thinking. Similar to a management system with a compliance objective, a management system with an innovation objective must have commitment and capability to develop innovation in sustainability. An organization needs to clearly define innovation. Without a clear definition, employees will not know the expectations. Recall from Chapter 1 that Beinhocker and Hanauer (2014) redefined capitalism, suggesting that prosperity or wealth for society is created by finding solutions to human problems. Finding solutions most likely would require finding a new approach or a change to the existing product, process, or procedure. If the current approach were working, then there would be no problems to solve. We have problems; therefore, change is required.

Porter and Kramer (2011) wrote an article entitled "Creating Shared Value" suggesting that companies can create economic value and social value simultaneously. They also suggest revisiting the characteristics of capitalism by "reconceiving products and markets," "redefining productivity in the value chain," and "enabling local cluster development." To be able to find solutions to human problems or create shared value, an innovation objective must be communicated to employees, responsibility for innovation should appear in employees' position descriptions, and employees must be rewarded for their innovations. Innovation will not happen unless capable people are hired with experience in innovation, and training is provided for employees. The organization structure needs to accommodate functional areas working together internally. Organizational alliances must also be developed externally with suppliers and customers to address innovative solutions to problems.

Companies might set up a dedicated budget for sustainability innovation in research and development (R&D) to signal their seriousness about addressing sustainability problems, but innovation does not have to occur just in R&D. Because sustainability is concerned with getting more out of each unit of resource (or simply put, becoming more efficient) and thereby reducing the impact on our planet, any change that creates efficiency would be innovative. Efficiency can occur by using less energy, consuming less water, or creating less waste in any of the following ways:

- redesigning processes used in the office, in production, in delivery, purchasing, or any number of steps in the value chain;
- retrofitting buildings;
- redesigning products or services offered to use fewer resources;
- turning waste materials into reusable materials; and
- working with suppliers, customers, and other stakeholders jointly to find solutions to new, less impacting products and a better world in which to live.

As companies look for opportunities for efficiency, they create cost savings that make them more competitive or develop new products for different markets.

Reflection: Innovation at Starbucks

Starbucks provides a Goals Summary in its Global Social Impact Performance Report including the goals, progress on the goals, and commentary. Are the goals solving society's problems and creating both social and economic value?

Area of Impact: Sourcing
Goal: 100 percent ethically sourced tea by 2020
Progress: 72 percent

Area of Impact: Greener Stores
Goal: Build and operate 10,000 greener stores globally by 2025
Progress: 1400 stores
Area of Impact: Foodshare
Goal: Rescue 100 percent of food available to donate by 2020 in U.S. company-owned stores
Progress: £3.5 million
Starbucks (2017, p. 21)

Key Takeaways

- A well-designed management system will connect an organization's policy (what it says it will do) with its performance (what it actually does).
- To fulfill sustainability objectives, governance is necessary at all levels of the organization including strategic (long-term), tactical (one year), and operational (day to day).
- A management system consists of both formal and informal elements working together.
- Commitment and capability must occur at all organizational levels of the management systems.
- To develop commitment, an organization communicates what is important, assigns responsibility for what is important, and rewards what is important.
- To develop capability, an organization provides resources, hires experienced people, trains internal employees, and creates opportunities for continuous learning.
- Management systems are designed for both compliance and innovation.

Innovation: Today's world is changing, and it's changing fast. At Air France-KLM, innovation and technology are two strong pillars in the integration of sustainability in the customer experience.

—Air France KLM (2017, p. 60)

CHAPTER 5

Indicators to Report Performance

Main purpose: Comprehend the role of indicators in sustainability reporting.

Objectives: After reading this chapter, you should be able to do the following:

- Recognize that quantitative performance requires qualitative discussion for interpretation.
- Develop a set of indicators that are appropriate for the policy of the organization.
- Assess indicators based on a set of characteristics *for indicators* and their appropriateness for a performance management system.
- Identify and classify different types of indicators.

Our board members asked us questions about the numbers. Then they told us where they would like to see the numbers. They are very much engaged in the reporting process . . . Having goals and targets and benchmarking will push us and other companies along that path.

—Anonymous Reporting Company

This chapter will help you to assess how an organization is performing against its intended actions. The intended actions are found in the policy statements and strategy documents (values, vision, mission, and related objectives and targets). The performance is reported in the sustainability reports. More specifically, in this chapter we focus on the indicators that are used to measure progress (Figure 5.1). Think of an indicator as a sensor that

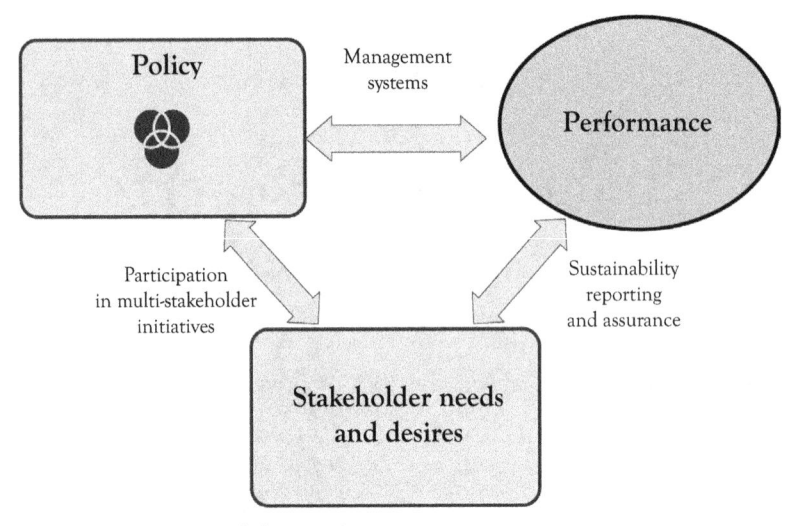

Figure 5.1 *Sustainability performance measurement*

Source: Based on Zenisek 1979

tracks, monitors, and assesses the progress or lack of progress on various aspects of sustainability and sends a signal to the report reader, similar to the instrument panel in an automobile. Although performance can be presented in qualitative or narrative form as well, when possible, organizations and their stakeholders usually prefer quantitative information. It allows them easily and quickly to assess trends, challenges, and accomplishments.

Quantitative Versus Qualitative Disclosure

For sustainability reporting, a performance measurement system includes the complete set of indicators (metrics, numbers, percentages, and monetary amounts) used to quantify how well an organization fulfilled its intentions as suggested in its policy statements. The indicators are a source of learning not only for external stakeholders but also for the internal stakeholders (management and other employees). See how Dell reports its progress in Figure 5.2.

In addition to the three sustainability dimensions (economic, social, and environmental), organizations may also be interested in reporting on other commitments they have made. Although the Global Compact and the Sustainable Development Goals (SDGs) fall under the broad umbrella of sustainability, often organizations will bring attention to the

Goal	Progress in FY18	2-year Trend	Progress to goal	Related SDGs
Supplier sustainability reports					
Ensure that Dell's suppliers representing 95% of direct materials spend publish a sustainability report in accordance with Global reporting Initiative (GRI) or equivalent recognized global framework	90%	In FY18, suppliers representing 90% of our direct materials spend published a sustainability report.	FY 18 — 90% FY 17 — 87% 0% 20% 40% 60% 80% 100% Percentage of direct suppliers with GRI reports	95%	Decent work and economic growth (8), reduced inequalities (10), responsible consumption and production (12)

Figure 5.2 Dell's FY 18 Legacy of Good: annual update on progress

Source: Reproduced with Permission of Dell Copyright © Dell 2019 (2019). ALL Rights Reserved.

indicators that apply to those specific commitments in their sustainability reports.

However, sometimes the numbers cannot tell the entire story. Just as a company's annual financial statements are accompanied by the Management, Discussion and Analysis and the Notes to the Financial Statements, sustainability reports should also contain narrative and notes to interpret the activities that are difficult to quantify or need further explanation. Quantitative indicators and qualitative discussion work together for an in-depth understanding of performance.

Reflection: Quantitative Indicators Versus Qualitative Discussion

Quantitative Indicators: Consider these as the instrument panel lights in an automobile or on a copy machine. The light will provide a warning that something could be wrong. However, a technical expert might need to investigate further to solve the problem.

Qualitative Discussion: Consider this as the conversation that you have with the technical expert regarding the warning light. It provides a deeper understanding of the problem and can explain why a positive or negative trend is occurring or what the company is doing to change the direction of the trend in the future.

Most companies provide a brief summary, similar to an instrument panel, at the beginning of the report, with additional detail and explanation later in the report. How does this format compare to the financial report?

Linking Indicators to Policy

As mentioned earlier, organizations develop indicators from the various topics that flow from the company's policy statements, which are developed through stakeholder engagement, especially the materiality process. The policy statements should also reflect material aspects, given the business model and context in which the company operates, such as the industry and region.

First time or young reporting companies are challenged to find the data in their systems necessary for the indicators. It takes time to develop information systems; however, that should not deter the company from beginning its sustainability reporting. The company might already have safety statistics, greenhouse gas (GHG) emissions/energy, and air quality information that are reported to an industry association or regulatory body. Likely, organizations already report donations, training costs, water use, and energy use in some form in the financial statements, and these items are good candidates for indicators. An organization can start small and their systems can evolve over time through continuous improvement. More indicators can be added to their systems once they have gained some experience in reporting.

Sustainability in Action: Connecting Policy and Indicators

Yes, we have aboriginal affairs policy. We have a stakeholders' relations policy, and we derive our indicators based on what we say in those policies.

I have a five-year strategy that I have put in place. Over the next five years we will make increases in the number of indicators that we report on.

—Anonymous Reporting Company

We learned that the Global Reporting Initiative's (GRI) reporting standards are the most widely recognized source for sustainability indicators. A multi-stakeholder group periodically updates the GRI Standards to meet the changing needs of stakeholders and the reporting entities. In contrast, some countries, such as China and Japan, create their own standards for sustainability reporting.

The GRI provides guidance for reporting for any type of entity: for-profit, nonprofit, governments and their agencies, and others. However, each industry and entity type has a different business model and operating context. Consequently, sometimes the general indicators do not fit the exact needs of the reporting organization in a particular industry. To customize the GRI standards for each industry, multi-stakeholder groups familiar with the industry work with industry representatives to develop appropriate indicators. The GRI Sector Disclosures are available on GRI's website.

GRI provides a broad set of indicators on economic, environmental, and social dimensions of reporting. Recall that other organizations provide more specific detail for reporting certain aspects of sustainability, such as GHG emissions. The Sustainability Accounting Standards Board, the Task Force on Climate-related Financial Disclosures, and the Climate Disclosure Standards Board all provide more detail on reporting of GHG emissions because many feel the topic is a top priority, especially for those companies that extract or use natural resources as part of their production system. Note how Canon, a leader in digital imaging solutions, also links its targets to the SDGs (Figure 5.3).

76 SUSTAINABILITY PERFORMANCE AND REPORTING

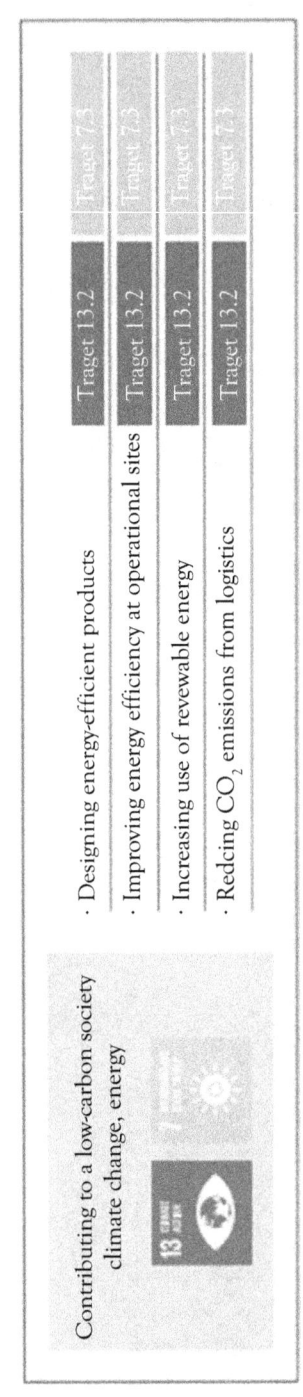

Contributing to a low-carbon society climate change, energy	· Designing energy-efficient products	Target 13.2	Traget 7.3
	· Improving energy efficiency at operational sites	Traget 13.2	Traget 7.3
	· Increasing use of revewable energy	Traget 13.2	Traget 7.3
	· Redcing CO_2 emissions from logistics	Traget 13.2	Traget 7.3

· Target 7.2: increase substantially the share of renewable energy in the global energy mix
Target 7.3: Double the global rate of improvement in energy efficiency
Target 13.2: Intergate climate change measures into national policies, strategies, and planning

Figure 5.3 Canon's initiatives and SDG targets

Source: Canon 2019

Characteristics of Good Indicators

If indicators are appropriate for reporting an organization's material topics, they will add credibility to the report. Also, using a standard set of indicators for an industry or sector supports credibility because they are more comparable. If indicators are difficult to interpret and understand, they might lead to a poor impression. Therefore, the choice of indicators is important. Organizations will look to their peer companies to determine which indicators they are using for certain aspects of sustainability. Whether reporting to external stakeholders or internal managers for monitoring and tracking progress, indicators should hold certain characteristics to ensure maximum learning. Possessing good indicator characteristics also supports better internal decision making. One set of characteristics uses the acronym *SMART*, which we will use here.

*S*pecific

*M*easurable

*A*chievable

*R*elevant

*T*imely

Let's understand how each of these characteristics applies to indicator development and selection.

Specific means that an indicator can pinpoint an action associated with a certain aspect of sustainability, and it is not confused with other aspects that can make the indicator invalid. The connection between the action measured and the indicator should be direct, clean, and clear, making it comparable to another company and understandable. Readers can interpret if the trend is going in the right direction. For example, if a company is attempting to measure employee satisfaction, the number of employee complaints or employee turnover is likely NOT specific to employee satisfaction. Employees who are dissatisfied might not be willing to register a complaint or an employee might leave his or her job because a family member needs help in a distant location. In contrast, many companies measure employee satisfaction with a survey to each employee using specific questions about satisfaction with their working conditions.

Reflection: Specific Indicators

GRI suggests that organizations report on the following two indicators:

(A) Total water withdrawal from all areas in megaliters.

(B) Ratio of basic salary and remuneration of women to men.

Are these two indicators sufficiently specific? Is there a way to make them more specific?

Measurable indicates that the data used to calculate the indicator are fairly easy to collect or are already collected in some form. An organization can also use a good proxy that represents the aspect to be measured. A proxy would be a stand-in or valid representative of the actual aspect. For example, it is impractical for an organization to measure actual climate change or temperature change; therefore, organizations measure GHG emissions instead. There is considerable evidence (although still some skeptics) that the amount of GHG emissions are linked to climate change. Because GHG emissions come from many different sources, it is also difficult to measure them directly through a gauge or meter such as water. Consequently, organizations use formulas to calculate the amount of GHG emissions based on the type and amount of fuel and electricity that was consumed because GHG emissions increase and decrease with energy used. Indicators are measurable when they are specific (previous characteristic). Therefore, having one characteristic might lead to ensuring other characteristics exist in the indicator as well. Even though GHG emissions are not highly specific or measurable, energy used is a good proxy and, for the most part, is specific and measurable. Despite the difficulty of measuring GHG emissions, they are very relevant and therefore an important indicator for organizations.

Reflection: Specific and Measurable Indicators

The specific and measurable characteristics are distinct, but they work together. Specific indicators are generally measurable. If indicators are derived from policies, then the policies must also be sufficiently specific.

To understand how these two aspects are interdependent, read this statement that was taken from an organization's environmental policy.

On an ongoing basis, we will act promptly to identify and correct any problems which pose an unacceptable threat to the environment.

Is the policy **specific** enough to measure the organization's **performance**?

Achievable means that the target behind the indicator can be reached. Good management of the indicator is critical to achieve the target. Similar to indicators that evaluate the performance of managers on purely financial performance, sustainability indicators should be within the ability of a management team if they have the appropriate commitment and capability (Chapter 4). Assigning an indicator to an employee's responsibilities helps to ensure commitment. If the indicator is showing a trend in the wrong direction, an employee should be capable of changing the direction of the indicator.

Be a critical thinker when looking at targets and their level of achievement. If Company A reports that it achieved its target and Company B reports that it did not, investigate if the targets were equally challenging for the two companies. Targets can be easy or challenging to achieve. Therefore, it is best to compare with another peer company's performance. Be sure if a company compares its performance to a benchmark that the benchmark represents a peer group of companies appropriate for comparison.

Sustainability in Action: Bank of America

Bank of America lists its Target, Target Year, Progress, and Status at the front end of its Environmental, Social, and Governance Performance Data Summary. This is one of the targets listed for environmental sustainability.

Target: $125 billion Environmental Business Initiative

Year: 2025

Progress: Since we launched this goal in 2013, we've provided more than $66 billion in financing for low carbon and other sustainable business. In 2017 alone, we delivered $17 billion toward this goal.

Status: On track

Is the target specific, measurable, and achievable?

Source: Bank of America (2017, p. 2)

Relevant means that the aspect of sustainability the indicator represents is important to the operations of the company and to its stakeholders (Chapter 3). If the organization's policy statements were prepared with stakeholder engagement, relevant indicators should evolve from the policy.

Timely means that the organization reports the indicator frequently enough to take corrective action, if necessary (hourly, daily, weekly, monthly or yearly). The indicator should act as a warning sign internally (e.g., a gas line leak). Externally, it should also be available for shareholders' timely decision making, usually every year. Schneider Electric provides timely updates on its performance similar to financial reporting (Figure 5.4).

SCHNEIDER SUSTAINABILITY IMPACT		Schneider Sustainability Impact 2018 –2020, Results as of Q1 2019					
			Objective 12/2019	Beginning 01/2018	Result Q4/2018	Result Q1/2019	
Our megatrends 2015 –2020 and targets 2018 –2020		Overall Score of 10	7/10	3	6.1	6.23	
CIRCULAR ECONOMY	75% of sales under our new Green Premium program			30.5%	45.7%	47.5%	
	200 sites labeled towards zero waste to landfill			140	178	178	★
	100% cardboard and pallets for transport packing from recycled or certified sources			50%	61.6%	77%	★
	120,000 metric tons of avoided primary resource consumption through ECOFITTM, recycling and take-back programs				43,572	49,538	
UP = Unpublished. Indicators amplified in Q1 2019 to upgrade Schneider Electric's sustainability ambitions marked with							★

Figure 5.4 Schneider Electric's quarterly update

Source: Schneider 2019

This completes the discussion of characteristics for SMART indicators. Before moving to indicator classification, let's see if we can improve a commonly used indicator.

Reflection: SMART Indicators

Some organizations use "total number and rate of employee turnover" as a social indicator to measure performance in labor practices. Can you think of a way to change the indicator to meet the SMART characteristics better?

Indicator Classification

There are several approaches to classify different types of indicators. Awareness of these classifications will help ensure that the performance measurement system is balanced and comprehensive. Some common classifications follow:

- economic, environmental, and social;
- input, output, outcome, and impact;
- efficiency and effectiveness;
- leading and lagging; and
- eco-efficiency and socioeconomic.

An indicator would rarely fit into just one of these classifications. For example, the amount of water used in a production system would likely be classified as an environmental input indicator and also a leading indicator. If the amount of water is divided by an output of production, such as cars serviced in a car wash, it could also be an efficiency or an eco-efficiency indicator.

Economic, Environmental, and Social Indicators

By this time, we should be familiar with the categories of economic, environmental, and social indicators. However, remember that a topic is not an indicator; consequently, a metric to measure the topic must be developed. Possible metrics for a few topics in each category follow, but these are only a few of the possibilities.

- *Economic indicators*: dollar of economic value distributed, percentage of goods purchased locally, percentage of taxes paid, and percentage of independent directors on the board of directors (often considered as an economic indicator or as separate category of sustainability, as in ESG).
- *Environmental indicators*: tons of GHGs and air emissions, number or volume of spills, tons of wastes, kilowatts of energy used, and tons of water used.
- *Social indicators*: percentage of employee turnover, number of injuries, hours of training, number of infractions of codes of conduct, and number of minorities in top management positions.

Input, Output, Outcome, and Impact Indicators and Measurability. Indicators can be classified as input, output, outcome, or impact.

- An input indicator will measure *what is going into a process*, such as dollars invested into a community, but it does not determine what result occurred with those dollars.
- An output indicator measures *what is coming out of a process*, such as number of food bank meals provided.
- An outcome considers the *short-term effects of the input or output*, such as satisfaction or enjoyment of the individuals eating the meals, and it might address if the meals were tasty and nutritionally balanced. Outcomes are important but are sometimes difficult to measure.
- Impact is *similar to outcome but considers the long-term effects* (both direct and indirect) from the dollars invested in the community program, such as health effects or better quality of life.

Although the definitions seem straight forward, input, output, and outcome classifications depend on a clear description of where a process starts and where it ends. The output or outcome of one process might be the input of another process.

Sustainability in Action: Marriott International Input, Output, Outcome, and Impact

Marriott International, a global hospitality company, indicated that by 2025 the company has committed "to invest at least $5 million to increase and deepen programs and partnerships that develop hospitality skills and opportunity among youth, diverse populations, women, people with disabilities, veterans, and refugees" (p. 41).

The indicator of $5 million investment most likely would be an input indicator. Elsewhere in the report, Marriott reported that it hired over 100 refugees through the International Rescue Committee. Hiring 100 refugees might be an output indicator associated with the investment. Marriott also reported that it held refugee hospitality training program in San Diego and Dallas. With this additional information, Marriott might call this a new process and the hiring would be the input indicator and the training the output indicator. If so, what then could be the outcome or impact that could be related to the hiring and training of refugees?

Source: Marriott International (2018)

When reviewing the indicators that an organization provides in its sustainability reporting, keep in mind that the ability to measure the input, output, outcome, and impact will sometimes determine the selection of the indicator. The ability to measure will also affect whether a quantitative indicator or a qualitative discussion is provided on a topic.

Figure 5.5 connects input and output with the ability to measure to determine the best type of indicator or procedure to use. To keep the figure simple, the table does not include outcome or impact but these terms can easily be substituted for output in regard to ability to measure.

Let's review some examples of the types of indicators that fit into each of the quadrants.

(a) *Input and output are both easy to measure.* A good example of measuring an input and output is training for safety prevention (input) and also measuring number of injuries (output). These indicators could also be classified as leading and lagging indicators (discussed later).

84   SUSTAINABILITY PERFORMANCE AND REPORTING

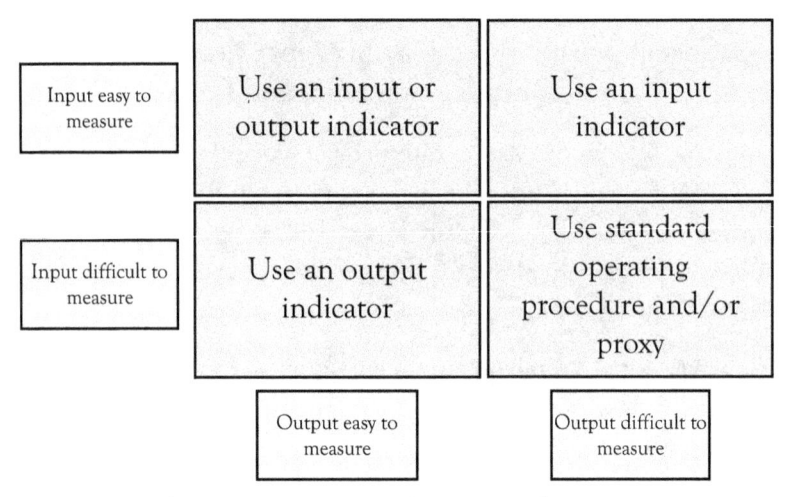

	Output easy to measure	Output difficult to measure
Input easy to measure	Use an input or output indicator	Use an input indicator
Input difficult to measure	Use an output indicator	Use standard operating procedure and/or proxy

Figure 5.5 Selection criteria for performance indicators

(b) *Input is easy to measure; output is difficult.* Dollars of investment in the community (input) is often used as an indicator because the actual output from the dollars invested is difficult to measure or too costly to monitor. In addition to accounting for the dollars invested, companies will often have terms of reference stating the types of projects and organizations that qualify for funding, which controls to some extent the output. To carry on the earlier example, if Marriott donated dollars to scholarships for education in hospitality, then it is possible to measure the output such as "number of students receiving scholarships" or the outcome of "number of students graduating and working for the company because of the scholarship program."

(c) *Input is difficult to measure, output is easy.* A company might want its employees to maintain a balance between work and other life activities. The input for each employee is difficult to track and maintain, especially those earning salaries, unless they keep a journal each day, which is onerous and potentially inaccurate. Instead, the company might opt for an employee satisfaction survey that asks about balance between work and other life activities.

(d) *Input and output are both difficult to measure.* Corruption is difficult to measure either as an input or output measure; therefore, companies try to rely on developing a strong ethical culture through codes of conduct, strong values, and other formal and informal procedures which act as standard operating procedures for employees. Some companies rely on 800 numbers to encourage employees to call and leave an anonymous message if they see something suspicious. They rely on these calls as a proxy for the ethical culture within the organization.

Look for a mixture of input, output, outcome, and impact indicators in an organization's sustainability reports to understand fully the various aspects of their activities. If the topic is important but difficult to measure, organizations will use a number of different indicators, hoping that they capture the effects of the activity.

Efficiency and Effectiveness Indicators

In broad terms, indicators represent progress or lack of progress in terms of efficiency and effectiveness. Efficiency indicators often lead to cost savings and therefore are consistent with improved financial performance. Some indicators use the ratio of input to output, which is a measure of efficiency. If just outcome or impact is of concern, then effectiveness indicators are used. They determine the extent that an objective was accomplished and the change that it made, regardless of cost. See Table 5.1 for a summary of efficiency and effectiveness indicators.

Table 5.1 Efficiency and effectiveness compared

Efficiency (output/input)	Effectiveness (outcome or impact accomplished)
What quantity of resources (input of labor and materials) did the company use to reduce a certain environmental impact such as GHG emissions (output)?	How well does a certain technology reduce GHG emissions?
What quantity of resources (input of labor and materials) did the company use to produce a certain quantity of products (output)?	How many repeat or satisfied customers came from the products the company produced?
How many hours of work (input) did the company use to increase the animal diversity in a certain region (output)?	How well does each of the company's procedures preserve biodiversity?

Other indicators use the ratio of input to outcome to measure more thoroughly the cost effectiveness (both efficiency and effectiveness) of certain activities. Cost effectiveness indicators answer the following questions:

- Which technology provides the greatest reduction of GHG emissions at the least cost?
- Which products are most satisfying to our customers and cost the least to produce?
- Which procedures provide the greatest biodiversity at the least cost?

Sustainability in Action: Baxter

Baxter, a health care company, reports Goals and Progress in its Sustainability Report:

Goal: Drive highest integrity and compliance to achieve zero government enforcement actions over compliance issues.

Progress: Baxter had zero corruption-related enforcement actions in 2017.

Is this an efficiency or effectiveness indicator?

Source: Baxter (2017, p. 7)

We now move to measuring efficiency and effectiveness. A couple of examples are provided.

Efficiency indicators use metrics such as the quantity of resources (input) to produce some product or service (output) such as energy per computer produced. For example,

$$\frac{\text{Kilowatts of energy consumed}}{\text{Number of computers produced}} = \text{Energy used per computer produced}$$

Effectiveness indicators use metrics to determine if the organization accomplished an objective, regardless of cost, such as achieving an absolute level of customer satisfaction, given the computers produced. For example,

Percent of Customers Very Satisfied, Satisfied, Dissatisfied, Very Dissatisfied

Reflection: Efficiency and Effectiveness

Question: Recall that input/output measures efficiency. How could you change the output indicator "number of homeless persons provided shelter" into an efficiency indicator?

Question: What type of indicator might determine if the meals provided sufficient nutrition or were tasty?

Leading and Lagging Indicators

Organizations will also consider the criticalness of an activity such as safety when deciding on the best type of indicator or indicators. An organization should collect data on input indicators for safety, such as "percentage of employees trained" or "percentage of employees wearing proper safety clothing" and also an output or outcome indicator, such as "number of injuries or fatalities." Therefore, one indicator should be used before an activity occurs (cause) and another indicator should be used to measure the aftermath (effect) to determine if the upfront procedures are working properly. Examples are provided in Figure 5.6.

- Input measures are similar to leading indicators (e.g., preventive indicators or controls used before an activity occurs).

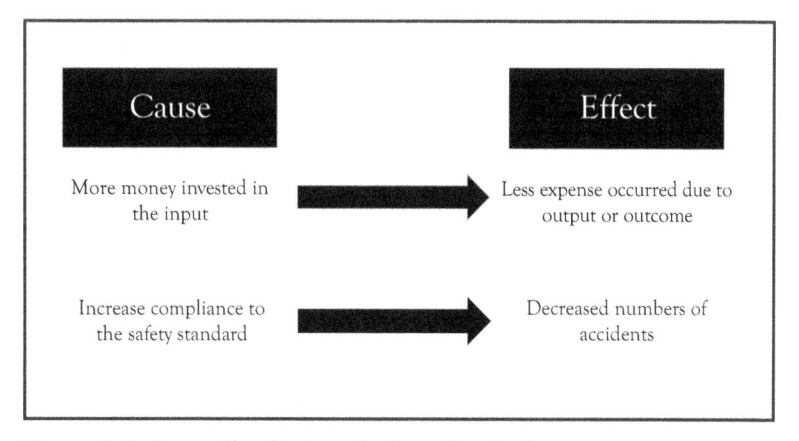

Cause	Effect
More money invested in the input	Less expense occurred due to output or outcome
Increase compliance to the safety standard	Decreased numbers of accidents

Figure 5.6 Cause (leading) and effect (lagging)

- Output or outcome indicators are similar to lagging indicators (e.g., detective indicators used after an activity happens).

Eco-Efficiency or Socioeconomic Indicators

Eco-efficiency (also called cross-cutting) indicators measure both economic and environmental performance with one dimension as the numerator and the other as the denominator. Likewise, socioeconomic indicators would measure both social and economic performance. Eco-efficiency cross cuts environment with economic, and socioeconomic cross cuts social with economic. However to add confusion, sometimes the term "social" is used to include both environmental and social. An eco-efficiency water indicator determines which organization can provide the most products with the least amount of water or cause the least amount of damage to the natural resource. Using fewer resources reduces the cost to produce the product and makes the organization more competitive.

To compare efficiency, an indicator must be normalized, which means it should be divided by some measure of production or size for better

$$\frac{\text{Liters of water}}{\text{Number of computers produced}} = \text{Liters of water used per computer}$$

comparison. The calculation above accomplishes this by dividing liters of water by the number of products. Obviously, larger organizations will have greater absolute impacts than smaller organizations. Generally, for better comparison indicators should be in one of the following forms: ratios, percentages, per capita, or per product.

Note, however, that reporting of GHG emissions is an exception to the normalization rule. Along with reporting GHG emissions per product produced (intensity), organizations should also report absolute emissions. Intensity could be decreasing but because the organization is growing its production, absolute emission can be increasing. All entities working together need to do their part to decrease their absolute emissions (Figure 5.7).

Another way to improve comparability is to show indicators against some benchmark, such as an industry average. In this way, the reader can get a sense for whether the organization performs above or below the average or standard (Chapter 6).

INDICATORS TO REPORT PERFORMANCE   89

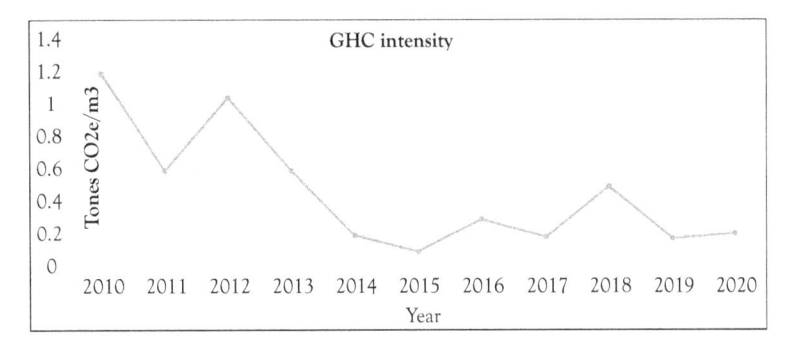

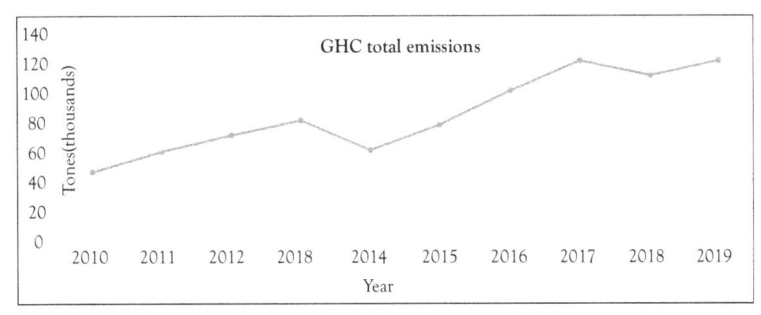

Figure 5.7 Intensity versus absolute GHG emissions

Sustainability in Action: WBCSD and Eco-Efficiency

The World Business Council for Sustainable Development (WBCSD) describes **eco-efficiency** as doing more with less. In practice, producing a product with smaller quantities of natural resources makes good business sense. Eco-efficiency might result in

- higher productivity due to the less waste creation and clean-up,
- increased competitiveness due to cost savings,
- improved reputation from environmental practices,
- reduced risk and liability from environmental contamination,
- increased revenue by developing innovative products from waste.

Source: DeSimone and Popoff with WBCSD (2000)

Key Takeaways

- Similar to financial accounting, narrative qualitative discussion helps to enhance disclosure of sustainability performance and to interpret the quantitative indicators.

- Companies often use footnotes in their sustainability reporting, similar to those in financial reporting, but less extensive.
- The policy and the stakeholder engagement process identify important topics for reporting performance; metrics in the form of indicators report performance.
- SMART indicators have the following characteristics: specific, measurable, achievable, relevant, and timely. Other sets of characteristics will have similar terms, but might not be exactly the same.
- Topics that are material fall into the categories of economic, environmental, and social; metrics to form indicators must be determined for each of the topics in each of the categories. A good source for indicators is the GRI Reporting Standards.
- A company should use a good mix of input, output, outcome, and impact indicators to develop a comprehensive performance measurement system. However, the degree of use of each type of indicator depends on the measurability.
- Input/output represents efficiency; outcome and impact represent effectiveness.
- Using both an input and output indicator for different phases of the same activity, such as safety training and number of injuries, result in leading and lagging indicators if there is a strong cause and effect relationship.
- Eco-efficiency or socioeconomic indicators are cross-cutting indicators that select a numerator from one dimension and a denominator from another dimension.

Sustainability engagement helped drive nearly $160 million of new revenue. We have long known that our Living Progress plan is the right thing for a responsible company to do. But we now have increasing evidence that our sustainability credentials contribute to our business objectives and deliver value to our shareholders.

—Hewlett Packard (2017, p. 66)

CHAPTER 6

Credible Reporting

Main purpose: Comprehend what qualities in a report make it credible in the eyes of the stakeholders.

Objectives: After reading this chapter, you should be able to do the following:

- Comprehend why companies and their sustainability reports are sometimes considered untrustworthy.
- Compare sustainability characteristics to financial reporting characteristics.
- Identify characteristics that support the credibility of sustainability reporting.
- Identify characteristics that detract from the credibility of sustainability reporting.

> *Trust is the intangible asset that can help assure the long-term sustainability of any organization or enterprise.*
> —William G. Parrett

In Chapter 3, we learned the importance of stakeholder engagement to connect an organization's policy to the needs and desires of stakeholders, ensuring the right sustainability direction for the organization. In Chapter 4, we comprehended how the policy links to performance through the management system that the organization develops. A policy is only a plan until committed and capable employees implement the plan through the management systems. Employees' activities at all levels (strategic, tactical, and operational) provide sustainable results. In Chapter 5, we determined that these results are then reported to the organization's stakeholders through various forms of sustainability reporting using a performance measurement system with a set of indicators. The most common reporting is either a stand-alone sustainability report or an integrated report, which includes results of the organization's performance in the dimensions of economic, environmental, and social. We also learned that organizations receive requests for more detailed information on certain aspects of sustainability (such as water, forestry, carbon, conflict minerals, to name a few) from governments, regulators, institutions, and others.

If an organization puts forth great effort to provide sustainability reporting, its disclosure should be believable and trustworthy, but many organizations make mistakes that undermine credibility. Common mistakes occur when organizations communicate in the wrong tone, include too many photos unrelated to operations, or create too rosy of a story. Consequently, stakeholders sometimes question the credibility of sustainability reports. In this chapter, we learn how to make sustainability reporting credible (Figure 6.1). The focus of this chapter is on the linkage between performance and stakeholder needs and desires.

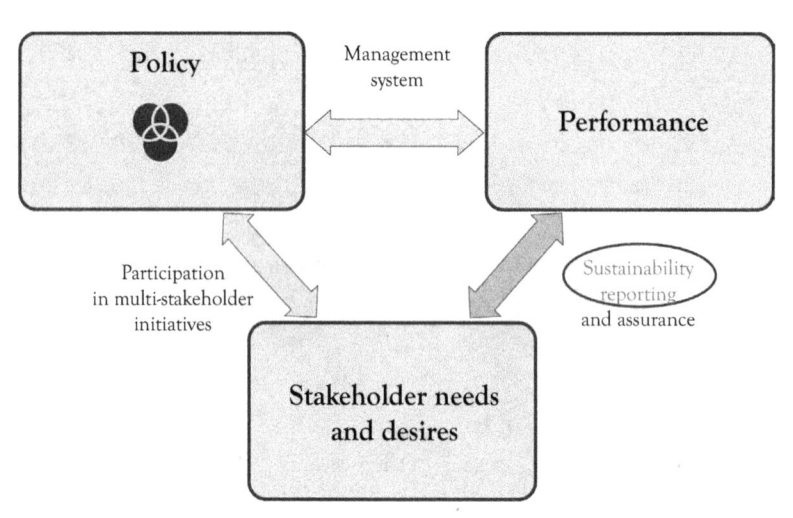

Figure 6.1 Sustainability reporting

Source: Based on Zenisek 1979

Trust in Reporting

Trust in business over the past years has generally been quite low; therefore, a lack of trust carries over to companies' sustainability reporting. From where does this lack of trust come? Because corporate mistakes, corruption, and social and environmental disasters are frequently in the headlines of the news and social media, society perceives the misgivings of one company to exist in all companies. According to the latest 2019 Edelman Trust Barometer, over 73 percent of respondents felt that focusing on sustainability does not have to be at the expense of profits. Unfortunately, the respondents also felt that many companies have not taken up this focus to the extent that they should (Edelman Trust Barometer 2019). When society feels that companies should act in a certain manner and they make promises through their policies to do so, but they are not upheld through their performance, it creates distrust.

Consequently, companies need to prepare sustainability reports carefully, incorporating characteristics that make them credible. Readers need to watch for characteristics that signify that the organization has carried through on its policy and objectives. Therefore, we learn in this chapter how to make sustainability reporting credible.

Critics of sustainability reports often use the terms "greenwash" and "spin" with reference to companies' sustainability performance or reporting. These words are commonly used to describe information that is perceived to be inaccurate, misleading, or unreliable. Think of a wall painted green and then use a knife to scrape away the green paint. Likely, it will be very thin and another color or bare surface will show. This is what is meant by greenwashing. It is a facade or cover-up of the company's true performance. Greenwashing more specifically refers to environmental performance that portrays an organization in a favorable manner or has the appearance of being green, when it really has done little to lessen its impact on the environment. Spin is a more general term that could apply to either environmental, social, or economic aspects of sustainability or even the financial reporting of an organization.

Sustainability in Action: Detecting Spin and Greenwash

We have to be careful that we are not spinning. It is hard to detect it yourself. Having an external party read the report helps.
—Anonymous Reporting Company

Originally, companies used the public relations function to communicate an organization's mission statement and values to the public. The purpose was to develop honest relationships with stakeholders, but more recently the word public relations seems to leave a negative impression and might suggest "spin." Spin means that circumstances or the reporting of the circumstances have any of the following characteristics:

- presented in a biased, not a balanced manner;
- has certain material or important details missing;
- promotes a misleading perception; or
- conveyed in a manner that draws attention to the positive and minimizes the negative aspect.

Reflection: Spin and Resumes

Robin is preparing a resume for a job interview. Of course, Robin wants to emphasize her strengths and de-emphasize her weaknesses. Robin has a bad habit of frequently being late for appointments. She will not include that information on her resume. Is she spinning?

Some critics believe that companies intentionally set out to mislead readers, whereas others attribute the lack of credibility to inexperience. Whatever the reason, as a reader or a preparer of a sustainability report, it is important to be aware of different procedures and practices that organizations can use to instill confidence in the reader that the report is as honest and accurate as possible. A company incurs considerable cost to publish a sustainability report, but if the report is not believable, the company will not maximize the potential benefits.

Characteristics of Credible Reporting

Similar to financial accounting, sustainability reporting has a set of qualitative characteristics in its conceptual framework that provides guidance to report in a credible manner. Also similar to financial statements, sustainability reports will contain many estimates to provide relevant and useful information to the reader, which sometimes gives the impression of inaccuracy. Companies would like their reports to possess positive characteristics, but due to lack of extensive experience in reporting, different value sets, and the sophistication of companies' information systems, not all reports give a credible impression.

CREDIBLE REPORTING 95

C = Defining report content; Q = Ensuring report quality

Sustainability Reporting GRI and Integrated Reporting Standards	Financial Reporting IASB/IFRS and US FASB
(C) Stakeholder Inclusiveness (C) Sustainability Content (Engagement: C. 3)	Relevance
(C) Materiality (Engagement: C. 3)	Materiality
(C) Completeness (Q) Accuracy (Assurance: C. 7) (Q) Balance	Faithful Representation
(Q) Comparability	Comparability
(Q) Reliability (Management Systems: C. 4)	Verifiability
(Q) Timeliness (Performance Indicators: C. 5)	Timeliness
(Q) Clarity (Performance Indicators: C. 5)	Understandability

Figure 6.2 Reporting characteristics

Figure 6.2 briefly compares financial reporting to sustainability reporting characteristics. Table 6.1 provides more detail on the characteristics.

Table 6.1 Comparison of sustainability and financial reporting characteristics

Sustainability Reporting: GRI/IR	Financial Reporting IFRS/FASB
Stakeholder Inclusiveness and Sustainability Content: stakeholder feedback on material topics and the sustainability process based on the organization's operations.	**Relevance:** financial information capable of making a difference in decision making.
Materiality: aspects that substantively influence assessments and decisions of stakeholders regarding the economic, environmental, and social activities.	**Materiality:** information that could influence decisions about a specific reporting entity.
Completeness and Accuracy: sufficiently accurate and detailed to assess performance with measurement techniques, estimates, and underlying assumptions disclosed. **Balance:** reflect both favorable and unfavorable performance aspects, results, and trends.	**Faithful Representation:** information is as complete, neutral, and free from error as possible.
Comparability: presents information consistently to analyze changes over time and to allow comparisons to other organizations directly or through the use of benchmarks.	**Comparability:** identification and understanding of similarities and differences among items; consistency helps to achieve that goal.

Reliability: subject to an examination that establishes the quality and materiality of the information within acceptable margins of error.	**Verifiability:** different knowledgeable and independent observers would come to the same results (within a certain range).
Timeliness: on a regular schedule and available when needed to influence decision making.	**Timeliness:** available in a period of time to influence decisions.
Clarity: understandable to stakeholders who have a reasonable understanding of the organization and its activities.	**Understandability:** presented clearly and concisely for someone with a reasonable knowledge of business and economic activities.

Sources: GRI (2018), IIRC (2013), IASB (2010), and FASB (2010).

GRI distinguishes between characteristics to define report content (stakeholder inclusiveness, sustainability context, materiality, and completeness) and to ensure report quality (balance, comparability, accuracy, timeliness, and clarity and reliability). IFRS/IASB distinguishes between fundamental qualitative characteristics (relevance with materiality as a subpart and faithful representation including complete, neutral, and free from error) and enhancing qualitative characteristics (comparability, verifiability, timeliness, understandability).

Characteristics that Support Credibility

We discussed stakeholder inclusiveness, context, and materiality thoroughly (Chapter 3); therefore, they are covered only briefly here. Other characteristics that support credibility are completeness, balance, accuracy, reliability, and comparability, which are discussed more thoroughly.

Stakeholder Inclusiveness, Stakeholder Context, and Materiality. Recall that Teck identifies topics that are material to its company: topics that rate high on both (a) significance to its stakeholders and (b) impact on the company. The topics rating high on both significance and impact should be integrated into the management system and the reporting. Therefore, note in Figure 6.3 how Teck links its reporting to the material topics identified by stakeholders (Teck's materiality matrix provided in Figure 3.5).

Materiality affects all the following decisions:

- which indicators to present individually and which indicators to aggregate with others;
- which indicators to have checked for accuracy; and
- where to place information that is material to some stakeholders but not others.

2017 Key Performance Indicators

Indicator
% of women working at Teck

Indicator
% of total employee turnover

Target
Increase % of women at Teck

Target
Keep total employee turnover under 10% each year

17% women

9% turnover

Learn More: Page 77

Learn More: Page 74

Figure 6.3 Teck: Linking indicators to material topics
Source: Teck 2017

Completeness. If a report is complete, it contains all the information that is necessary to make good decisions about an organization's sustainability performance; therefore, it is also related to materiality. However, stakeholders' information needs may differ. That is why companies often provide the topics that are relevant to different stakeholder groups in their stakeholder engagement section of the report. It is difficult to provide a complete report that is also brief and concise and does not overwhelm readers with too much information. Sustainability reports can often contain over 100 pages, especially for the more impacting companies in the resource extractive industries. What can companies do to satisfy the completeness requirements but also keep the length of the document within reason? If the report has been prepared according to GRI, there should be a GRI Index. Notations often appear in the index or some place in the report that additional information can be found elsewhere and where it can be found. For example, governance information is located in the Proxy Statement for the Annual General Meeting and therefore companies refer readers to this document for the information or to their website. Figure 6.4 provides an example of part of Alma Media's GRI Index. Alma Media is a media company.

Additional Information in Governance Documents		
GRI Indicator		Location
102-28	Evaluating the highest governance body's performance	Corporate Governance Statement p.10
102-30	Effectiveness of risk management processes	Report by the Board of Directors and Financial Statements pp18-19
102-32	Highest governance body's role in sustainability reporting	p.7

Additional Information in Code of Conduct	
Principle	Locations
Principle 2: Businesses should make sure that they are not complicit in human right abuses	Code of Conduct, pp. 21-23,31
Principle 10: Businesses should work against corruption in all its forms, including all extortion and bribery	Code of Conduct, p.21- 23

Figure 6.4 Alma media's GRI index

Source: Alma Media 2018

For our purposes, a report that is complete will have the following characteristics:

- *Materiality:* includes all topics that are significant to stakeholders and have a high impact on the company;
- *Balance:* contains both accomplishments and challenges; and
- *Comparability:* allows assessment of performance against similar organizations and operations.

We can see that these characteristics are interdependent. Fulfilling one characteristic often helps to fulfill another. We discuss both balance and comparability next.

Balance. Balance means reporting the accomplishments along with the challenges. You might ask why organizations do not report more information about their challenges or what they did not accomplish. There are likely several reasons, but regardless of whether an individual or an entity, no one likes to discuss perceived failures. In addition, the media tend to focus on negative information about organizations; therefore, managers sometimes rationalize that their sustainability reports provide them with an opportunity to tell the other side. As well, some legal departments fear that providing information on what the company should have done, but did not accomplish, might lead to legal suits against the company.

Nevertheless, providing an unbalanced narrative would surely lead to the perception of greenwashing and distrust of the company's performance.

CREDIBLE REPORTING 99

Consequently, the report should provide both negative and positive aspects, and the negative aspects should not be hidden in the report or difficult to find. However, rarely will the reader see a section in the report titled BAD NEWS. Often times the reader can detect negative aspects when a company indicates it did not make sufficient progress on an initiative, when the numbers show a trend in the wrong direction, or when the company discusses challenges that it faces. Be alert to negative aspects in the sustainability report in various sections throughout the report. The examples from Domtar and Marks and Spencer (M&S) show different approaches to providing balance in their reports. M&S is straightforward in showing that many of its initiatives toward its goals have not been implemented yet (Figures 6.5 and 6.6).

Wellbeing	Not started	Not achieved	Behind plan	On plan	Achieved
Colleague wellbeing framework	●		●		
Colleague health assessment	●				
Wellbeing in employability	●				
Mental health training				●	
Health and safety data					

Emissions	Not started	Not achieved	Behind plan	On plan	Achieved
Science based target emissions				●	
Carbon neutral operations				●	

Figure 6.5 M&S performance summary (Balance)

Source: Marks & Spencer (M&S) 2018

PRIORITIES

Managing our water use in a way that helps maintain the quantity, quality, timing and distribution of local water resources.

Understanding the full cost of using water to empower local facility managers to use it more efficiently.

Sharing best practices for improving the efficiency and effectiveness of our wastewater treatment systems.

CHALLENGES

Bringing all water users together to develop a more integrated and equitable approach to improving and protecting water quality at the watershed level.

Understanding water flows within our older mills where water meters are more limited and not ideally located.

Maintaining performance given aging equipment and capacity constraints in several of our wastewater treatment systems.

PROGRESS

Conducted pilot studies at three mills to determine the appropriate cost elements, flows and methods needed to build a model to better understand the full cost of using water.

Decreased total water use in our pulp and paper mills 5 percent, and decreased discharges of AOX 11 percent, BOD 2 percent and TSS 10 percent since 2012.

11% REDUCTION IN AOX DISCHARGES AT PULP AND PAPER MILLS SINCE 2012

2% REDUCTION IN BOD DISCHARGES AT PULP AND PAPER MILLS SINCE 2012

10% REDUCTION IN TSS DISCHARGES AT PULP AND PAPER MILLS SINCE 2012

Figure 6.6 Domtar's priorities, challenges, and progress

Source: Domtar 2017

In comparison, view Figure 6.6 and how Domtar provides its Priorities, Challenges, and Progress.

Balancing favorable with unfavorable performance has been found to be one of the characteristics most important for credibility in a report. After all, just as we are all human and make mistakes, so do organizations. Therefore, it is important that an organization admits its failings and indicates how it will turn the situation around.

Sustainability in Action: What Companies Say About Balance

If you read a report and it shows a balance of performance—both good and bad—then I take that report at face value. However, if it shows performance that is all good, I would seriously question that report. Well, finding the right balance [positive and negative] is very important for our report to be credible.

—Quotes from Reporting Companies

Accuracy and Reliability. Accuracy and reliability are related, as accurate information is also reliable information. If two different individuals do an analysis separately and they come up with the same result, it is assumed to be reliable. (Chapter 7 on assurances provides more information on this topic.) In general, companies do not intentionally put inaccurate information in their reports, but in an effort to meet the timeliness characteristic (release the report by its targeted delivery date), sometimes errors do occur. Some of the reasons might be the following:

- human error due to inexperience, carelessness, or fatigue;
- a change or improvement in the method of recording information;
- information systems with insufficient controls to ensure accuracy.

Sustainability in Action: Systems and Accuracy

Because our systems are pretty well developed, the quality of reporting is much higher. We are much more accurate now than we were about our impacts in the beginning.

—Anonymous Reporting Company

To ensure accuracy in their sustainability reporting is one of the reasons that organizations often have their internal auditor, external auditor, and a stakeholder advisory panel to review the report before it is published. In some companies, the board of directors also reviews the reporting.

Comparability. We discuss two procedures in this section that organizations use to make reports comparable: benchmarks and standards. Benchmarks can be used in several ways for comparison:

- year-to-year,
- progress with a target, and
- other companies in a similar line of business.

Year-to-year comparisons and reporting progress against a target are quite common in sustainability reports but comparing against peers is not. Nevertheless, readers often want to know how an individual company performed compared to its peers. Therefore, rating organizations have come into existence to benchmark peer companies against each other (discussed in Chapter 2). However, both M&S and Samsung provide good benchmarks in their reports. M&S shows its injury rate against several benchmarks, and Samsung has developed its own internal benchmark with the help of an externally accepted standard (Tables 6.2 and 6.3).

Table 6.2 M&S's health and safety benchmark

RIDDOR injury rate per 100,000 employees	Fatal	Specified	Over 3 or 7 days	Total
M&S UK retail	0	25	130(7)	155
2016/2017 HSE UK retail bench mark	0.11	48	172(7)	220
M&S warehouse	0	52	262(7)	314
2016/17 HSE UK warehouse benchmark	1.42	325	1252(7)	1577

Source: Marks & Spencer (M&S) 2018

Table 6.3 Samsung working hours benchmark

Working Hour Management[1]

	2015	2106	2017
Workweek average compliance[2]	89	83	87
Average weekly work hours	48	53	52
Maximum average weekly work hours	52	57	54
Average work hours of those who work 40 hours or more per week	52	55	54
Compliance with the guarantee of one-day off per week	89	94	97

Source: Samsung Electronics 2018

---

[1] Based on global suppliers

[2] A work week should not be more than 60 hours per week (RBA criteria)

Until organizations report a performance metric, such as toxic spills, using the same protocol or guideline and in the same units, the benchmark is useless. Not only must all organizations count the same items in the metric, but they must also be clear on its definition: For example, these questions arise regarding reporting of spills of a contaminated substance:

- Were spills measured by volume, number, or both?
- If by volume, how big was the spill before including it in the spill count?
- Which chemicals were considered toxic?

Sustainability in Action: Comparability in Different Jurisdictions

Volume in Reportable Spills: Jurisdiction A requires reporting incidents of spilled substances over 100 milliliters. Jurisdiction B requires reporting incidents of spilled substances over 1,000 milliliters. A company in Jurisdiction B could have 1,000 or more spills less than 1,000 milliliters, and none of them would be reported.

Reportable Substances: Company A reports the volume of all spills (oil and water) in a single metric, with 99 percent of the volume spilled consisting of water. Company B excluded water spills from the reportable substances. Company A's spill record appears extremely poor compared to Company B.

GRI Reporting Standards generally suggest to "use the definitions of the jurisdiction you're operating in …" meaning that thresholds and definitions of their sustainability metrics may differ due to different regulations.

Guidelines and standards help to make benchmarks reliable, helping with comparability. XBRL (eXtensible Business Reporting Language) is a global standard for exchanging business information. However, it is in the early stages of development. XBRL is used for some forms of financial reporting. Eventually, information found in sustainability reports will be XBRL enabled, which will standardize information and make it easier for the reader to compare organizational performance.

Sustainability in Action: Comparability

So there is a real challenge to having consistent reporting so that it is absolutely comparable between organizations, like financial information. It will take some time to have completely standardized reports from all companies because they are all tuned into their own "corporate culture," quite rightly.

—Anonymous Reporting Company

Other guidelines or standards that we discussed under reporting (Chapter 2) and management systems (Chapter 4) help to make reports comparable, such as CDP, GRI, SASB, and ISO. Even though the content and format of reports are becoming more standardized, lots of variation still exists. Sustainability reporters need more time and experience to become more comparable.

Reflection: Protocols for Accounting for GHG Emissions

Companies who report to the CDP provide the protocol (accounting method) that they are using to account for greenhouse gas (GHG) emissions. The CDP lists more than 60 protocols that are acceptable (CDP n.d.). Many organizations use several protocols to report emissions from different activities. A few are listed below and all of these are acceptable standards for reporting carbon or GHG emissions.

- IPCC Guidelines for National GHG Inventories, 2006
- The GHG Protocol: A Corporate Accounting and Reporting Standard (Revised Edition)
- United States Environmental Protection Agency (EPA) Mandatory GHG Reporting Rule
- Canadian Association of Petroleum Producers
- American Petroleum Institute Compendium of Greenhouse Gas Emissions
- ISO 14064-1
- The Climate Registry: General Reporting Protocol
- European Union Emission Trading System (EU ETS): The Monitoring and Reporting Regulation (MMR)—General guidance for installations

What does this mean for comparison?

Characteristics that Detract from Credibility

There are certain characteristics that are not inaccurate per se, but lead the reader to believe that the organization is dishonest and untrustworthy. Three are discussed here: careless illustrations, aggregated data, and imprecise/vague disclosure. You might be able to find others in sustainability reporting.

Careless Illustrations. Companies sometimes present graphs and charts in a confusing manner or with missing data. Compare the two graphs. Notice how compressed (first graph) or spread the intervals (second graph) are on the vertical axis, which gives the appearance that a greater change in waste occurred. On the horizontal axis of the first graph, the intervals (spread of the numbers) are not consistently spaced throughout the entire axis, creating a misleading picture, especially for the larger amounts (Figure 6.7).

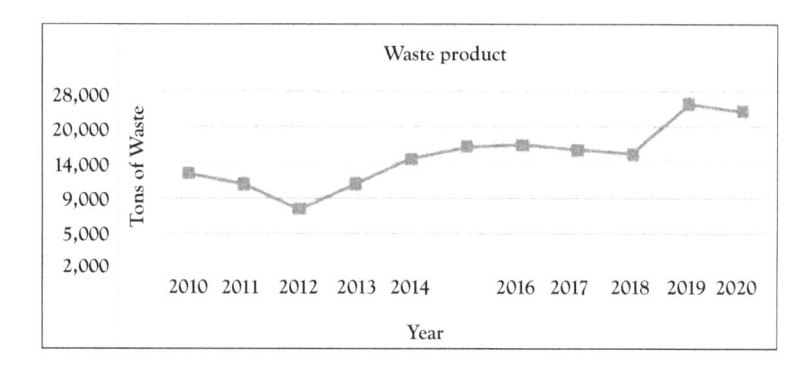

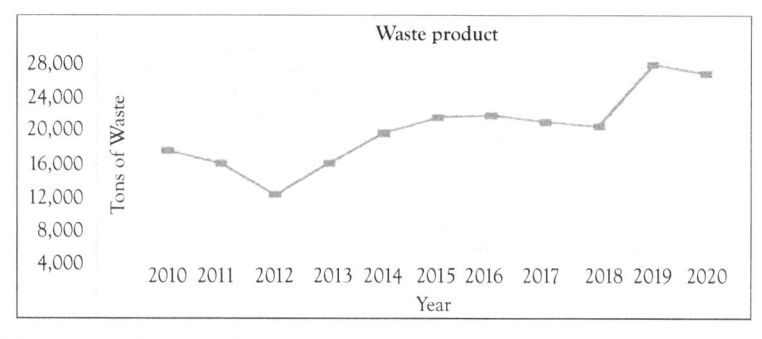

Figure 6.7 Careless illustrations

Aggregated Data. This process is similar to financial statement presentation. Often the results of operations statement (income statement) contains one line called "selling general and administrative expenses." This one line is a total of many, many expenses. Generally, more detail on these aggregated numbers can be found in the notes to the financial statements. Similarly, when reading a sustainability report, the reader might notice that the organization does not discuss a favorite topic or environmental condition and feels that the organization is attempting to hide something. Even though this indeed could be the situation, an alternative explanation is that management decided, due to space limitations, to aggregate the data with other numbers or place the data on the organization's website.

For example, some companies will aggregate contractor and employee safety rates. Contractors often have higher injury occurrences because riskier tasks are often contracted out to specialists, and the company has less control over contractors. To mitigate the problem, some companies require contractors to undergo the same training as employees. Therefore, isolating contractor and employee injury rates adds additional information. Figure 6.8 illustrates how Suncor's injury rates are disaggregated.

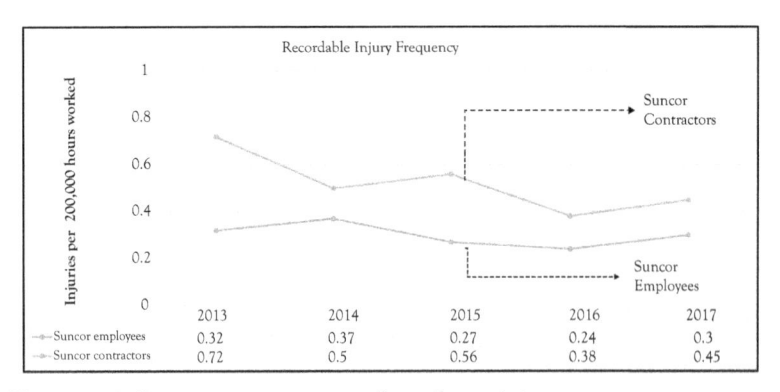

Recordable Injury Frequency

	2013	2014	2015	2016	2017
Suncor employees	0.32	0.37	0.27	0.24	0.3
Suncor contractors	0.72	0.5	0.56	0.38	0.45

Injuries per 200,000 hours worked

Figure 6.8 Suncor: contractor and employee injury rates

Imprecise and Vague Disclosure. Sometimes sustainability disclosure is not sufficiently detailed to understand the company's actions or the writing is too technical for the average reader to understand. Compare the excerpts that are vague and imprecise to those that are clear and specific and indicate which ones you feel are more credible.

Table 6.4 Disclosure: vague/imprecise or clear/specific

Vague and Imprecise	Clear and Specific
We have a hazardous waste avoidance plan and investigate how to decrease hazardous waste in the future.	We track hazardous waste on a daily basis. In the past year, our hazardous waste decreased by 10 percent. We have a hazardous waste team that reports options to decrease hazardous waste on a monthly basis.

Table 6.4 Disclosure: vague/imprecise or clear/specific (Continued)

All of our facilities are ISO 14001 certified.	All of our facilities have ISO 14001 certified environmental management systems. Our internal auditors check each facility's compliance on a two-year rotating basis. Facilities must report progress on eliminating any deficiencies within three months of the audit.
We have training programs for all of our staff, management, and field personnel.	Safety training hours averaged 2.5 hours for staff, 2.0 hours for managers, and 5.4 hours for field personnel. Ninety percent of the employees in these categories received training. Training appears to have reduced our injury rate by three percent this past year.

Key Takeaways

- Sustainability reports need to embody certain qualities to make them credible, including engagement with stakeholders (stakeholder inclusiveness) to determine which topics are most important to them (materiality) and which topics have the greatest impact on the company (sustainability context).
- When there appears to be a gap between a company's promises and their delivery, credibility is questioned, unless the company explains why the difference has occurred.
- The characteristics that make financial reporting credible and useful are similar to the characteristics that make sustainability reports credible and useful.
- Many of the characteristics are interdependent; for example, complete reports contain topics that are material, balanced, and comparable.
- Comparability allows for assessment of performance against similar organizations and operations; reporting results from year-to-year, against targets, and against benchmarks supports comparability.
- Using standards or guidelines help with comparability; however, different jurisdictions provide different protocols,

regulations, or units for reporting aspects of sustainability, which makes certain indicators less comparable.
- Companies should provide reports on a regular basis; many companies that do not provide an integrated report (social and environment integrated in the financial report) will attempt to release their sustainability report at the same time as their financial report.
- Assurances help to make reports reliable, which means two independent individuals will come to the same conclusion.
- Some characteristics that detract from credibility are careless illustrations, information that is too aggregated, or disclosure that is imprecise and vague.

The most essential quality for leadership is not perfection but credibility. People must be able to trust you.
—Rick Warren (2012, p. 253)

CHAPTER 7

Assurances

Main purpose: Comprehend the role of assurances in sustainability performance and the reporting of sustainability performance.

Objectives: After reading this chapter, you should be able to do the following:

- Identify assurances that give confidence to stakeholders that organizations are advancing their sustainability performance and that their reporting is an accurate reflection of their activities.
- Recognize the differences, strengths, and weaknesses between internal and external assurances.
- Compare limited and reasonable assurance characteristics.
- Interpret various characteristics of an assurance report found in a sustainability report.

There can be no great courage where there is no confidence or assurance, and half the battle is in the conviction that we can do what we undertake.

—*Orison Swett Marden*

Thus far, we have reviewed all the major dimensions of the sustainability model for organizations. We started with the stakeholders and their input into the policy of an organization. Organizations also participate in multi-stakeholder groups to develop a tight link between stakeholders' needs and desires and their policy. Then, we moved to the management systems, which develop a tight link between the organization's policy and its performance. The next dimension we studied was performance in which we learned approaches to ensure credibility in the eyes of both internal and external stakeholders through selection of appropriate indicators.

110 SUSTAINABILITY PERFORMANCE AND REPORTING

To develop a tight link between the organization's performance and stakeholders' needs and desires, organizations provide many forms of sustainability reporting. Our final topic is assurance, which often pertains to the accuracy of the performance metrics used for sustainability reporting. However, management might decide to provide more certainty to other aspects of the dimensions in the model for sustainability. Assurances help to give confidence that the linkages illustrated in the model for organizational sustainability are strong and working properly. (See Figure 7.1.)

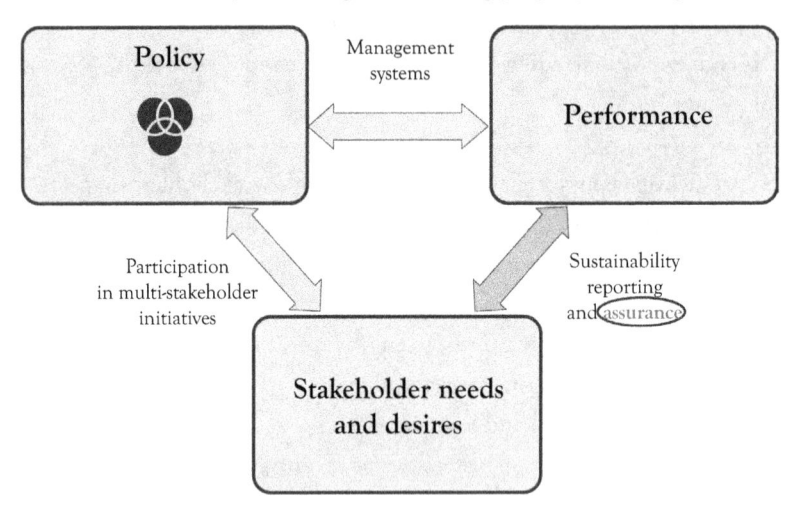

Figure 7.1 Assurances for sustainability reporting

Source: Based on Zenisek 1979

Various levels of management and the board of directors want assurance that the organization has the right processes and controls to link its policy statements to its actual performance. They also want to have confidence that the performance indicators provided in the sustainability report are representative of the organization's actual performance and that the report does not contain any material errors or omissions which may create legal or reputational problems for the company.

Confidence in Reporting

Assurance of any type provides confidence to the organization, as well as its stakeholders, that the information reported is "reasonably accurate," honest, and reliable for decision making. We use "reasonably" because the report contains many estimates, and an organization's sustainability progress can be reported using different standards/guidelines. In financial accounting, the term "faithful representation" is used in a similar manner. As well, the term "assurance" is used rather than audit because an audit is only one procedure used to provide assurance. Assurance is a broad, all-encompassing term that applies to the outcome of various types of reviews or verification processes, some of which are audits. It is helpful to think of assurance techniques on a spectrum indicating degree of rigor, with auditing as the most intensive and periodic checks as the least intensive.

Assurances let stakeholders know that the sustainability report fairly represents a company's performance, the same as financial assurances (usually called audits) do for the capital providers of publicly traded companies. However, unlike financial audits that have been around for many years and are standardized, assurance providers for sustainability reporting gained promience only since the early 2000s. Assurance providers had to learn how to assure this information by adapting their experience from financial audits. Initially, there were no guidelines available specifically for sustainability assurance, and assurance providers along with standard setting bodies had to develop them. Because assurance statements are new and still changing, not all the statements will have exactly the same information in the assurance statement. Furthermore, many types of organizations in addition to accounting firms provide assurance for sustainability reporting. Therefore, we discuss various approaches to provide assurance in this chapter.

Organizations use assurances in a number of different ways concerning sustainability. Assurances can be provided on the management system itself or any of its various components. Assurance procedures can also confirm that the company calculated its performance indicators in accordance with a certain standard, (e.g., the calculations for GHG emissions follow a certain protocol or standard or that reporting is compliant with the GRI Reporting Standards). Assurances help to determine if employees follow proper procedures and processes to support credible reporting. Internal or external personnel can perform the procedures necessary for assurance depending on the objective. Note the different types of assurances that Apple performed on its processes, performance, and report.

Sustainability in Action: Apple's Assurances and Review Statements

Apple uses two firms (see the report for more detail of audits and assurances).

Bureau Veritas

- Overall Assurance of Report (p. 60) including Processes and Selected Indicators
- Supplier Clean Energy Program (p. 67) including Processes and Selected Indicators

Fraunhofer Institute

- Comprehensive Carbon Footprint (p. 63) including Processes.
- Comprehensive Fiber Footprint (p. 70) including Processes and Selected Indicators.
- Packaging Plastic Footprint (p. 72) including Processes and one Indicator.

Are these assurances reliable?

Source: Apple (2018, pp. 62–74).

Internal Versus External Assurances

Both internal and external assurances improve the quality of information. Internal controls and internal audits (internal assurances), independent third-party reviews, and third-party commentaries (external assurances) all help to make information more credible and therefore more useful to the reader. Thus, everyone benefits. Assurances can do the following:

- enhance the readers' and the organization's confidence about the reported information;
- lead to better decisions or judgments about performance;
- allow others, not preparing the report, to provide valuable ideas on the interpretation and analysis of the report indicators; and
- provide the impetus to improve sustainability performance.

Similar to financial accounting, if a company has completed rigorous internal assurances, then the external assurance is less costly (for financial accounting, the term generally used is internal and external audit). Regarding internal assurances, a department or division within an organization that is knowledgeable about the subject matter usually performs a review or an audit on a sustainability activity that is the responsibility of another department or division. In contrast, an objective third party, knowledgeable about the sustainability aspect but not employed by the organization, performs an external assurance.

Processes for internal assurances are generally proactive and attempt to ensure that there is a system in place to aid in accomplishing objectives and to provide accurate and relevant reporting on the objectives. They also quickly help to identify problems occurring during an activity, such as a data collection process, and before the final sustainability report is prepared. On the other hand, processes for external assurances are generally reactive and identify inadequate reporting systems, errors, inaccuracies, or inadequate performance after an activity has occurred, such as after a report is prepared but before it is made available to the stakeholders. For an excellent comparison of internal versus external assurances regarding financial reporting, see Factsheet: Internal Audit versus External Audit (IIA Australia 2018).

Internal Assurance: Internal Controls and Internal Audits

There are many types of internal assurances. We learn two main categories and their relationship: internal controls and internal audits. Internal personnel work with both. Generally, internal assurances (both internal controls and internal audits) come from the internal auditing function within the company. For financial reporting, internal auditors are professionally trained in controls and audits. For sustainability controls or reporting, often a multidisciplinary team is created. An internal auditor who is professionally trained in auditing heads the team and other members from technical areas work together to help the board of directors and management with any of the following duties (IIA, n.d.):

- aid in the identification of material environmental and social risks and suggest how risks can be mitigated.

- determine if controls, processes, and procedures are adequate to support the objectives.
- provide insight for achieving objectives more efficiently and effectively.
- ensure accurate and relevant sustainability reporting through appropriate indicators.
- determine compliance with policies, commitments, laws, and regulations.

See Table 7.1 for a partial list of examples of the different types of internal assurances that Samsung uses. Note that the company clearly assigns responsibility for each of the assurances.

Table 7.1 Samsung: internal responsibilities for assurances

Category	Management system	Mandate	Responsibility units
Compliance	Compliance Program Management System (CPMS1)	Reporting of compliance violations, help desk, self-initiated reviews, posting of manuals and guides	Corporate Compliance Team, Global Privacy Office
Anti-corruption	Ethics Management System	Posting of the Management Principles and Code of Conduct, reporting of corrupt practices	Audit Team
Personal Information Security	Privacy Legal Management System (PLMS2)	Personal data protection management of products and services	Global Privacy Office
Intellectual Property Rights	IT4U	Ban on the illegal use of software	IT Strategy Group
Labor Relations	GHRP Portal	Compliance with labor standards, posting of HR regulations	HR Team
Environmental compliance	Global Environment, Health and Safety System(G-EHS3)	Environment & Safety of workplaces and products	Global EHS Center
Trade	Conflict Minerals Management System(TCS4)	Strategic resources, management of conflict minerals use	Corporate Compliance Team

Samsung Electronics, 2018, 103

Internal Controls. Recall that a management system consists of the entire set of policies, procedures, monitoring, and tracking mechanisms. Sometimes the term management system is expanded to management planning and control system to be more specific about what it does. Management systems and their controls can be specified by an external organization such as ISO 14001. Nevertheless, they must be developed internally and customized to meet the organization's needs. Internal controls can be both formal and informal. Commitment and capability tend to be informal controls and therefore more difficult for an auditor to determine if they are at the right levels. Regardless, they are extremely important, and certain types of controls can help support commitment and capability (Chapter 4). We briefly review the controls related to commitment and capability. Two very different companies, an energy company and a retail running shoe and apparel manufacturer, indicate the importance of internal controls for performance and reporting.

Sustainability in Action: ConocoPhillips and Nike

ConocoPhillips reports (ConocoPhillips, 2017, p. 53):
Our internal quality assurance process begins at the business unit level. This process includes

- *ensuring that business units understand the corporate reporting obligations associated with safety, health, and environmental metrics.*
- *establishing standardized methods of data collection and expected reporting procedures.*
- *verifying that the data provided by business units are accurate and complete.*
- *reviewing and questioning the results.*
- *assessing results to identify trends and better understand the drivers of year-over-year changes.*

Nike reports: (Nike 2016/17, p. 2)
Based upon a thorough review by NIKE's internal audit function, considerable progress has been made to NIKE's sustainability data processes over the past several fiscal years, including but not limited to:

- *a performance management data system overhaul,*
- *development of standard operating procedures, and*
- *an improved data governance model.*

The review also identified opportunities to further improve systems and controls around sustainability reporting. NIKE will continue to evolve and address information systems in light of this goal.

Both companies identified the importance of governance, not only at the highest levels (Nike) but also throughout the organization's business units (ConocoPhillips). Part of governance is assigning responsibility. However, ensuring accountability is much broader than just a formal assignment of job duties. Management establishes an informal culture of accountability within an organization by developing high expectations that employees will make ethical decisions even when formal controls cannot be established or performance monitored. Some controls that support accountability follow:

- electing members to the Board that have sustainability values and expertise;
- structuring the organization to give prominence to units responsible for sustainability;
- building rigorous systems to collect data that determines progress on objectives;
- ensuring sustainability indicators are given equal importance to financial indicators.

Part of the internal auditor's responsibilities is to identify control procedures necessary in various business units and help the employees in the unit to design and implement the procedures. The auditor helps the employees take responsibility for the continued use and maintenance of the controls to achieve the desired objectives. This approach helps with capability and commitment of the employees. Then, periodically the auditor will return to perform a review to determine if the controls are still appropriate and working.

Internal Audits. An internal audit is a more formal periodic and systematic review to determine "how well risks are managed including whether the right processes are in place, and whether agreed procedures are being adhered to" (IIA 2019). Internal auditors perform internal audits. They are employees of the organization being audited. An auditor should be independent of the subject matter he or she is auditing. As an employee of an organization that is receiving an audit, the internal auditor's independence is compromised to some degree. The auditors might hesitate to report that controls need to be improved for fear of losing their jobs. However, direct lines of reporting to top management and/or to the board of directors create more independence for the internal auditors. Internal auditors provide many benefits to an organization, especially early identification of potential problems; consequently, it benefits an organization to have a team of auditors working for the organization full time.

Internal auditors follow a set of professional standards to perform a review and provide an opinion on the subject matter of the audit. Similar to setting up internal controls, a multidisciplinary audit team, headed by a professionally trained auditor, will carry out the audit. Technical expertise is also needed. For example, the auditor might not be familiar with the regulations and calculations specific to GHG emissions. Therefore, an engineer with experience on emissions calculations will likely join the team. Teams of auditors review internal controls to ensure they are still appropriate if the operating environment has changed. They also check to ensure that employees are following the controls that are in place and not by-passing them. The team will make recommendations for improvements if they identify weaknesses.

Sustainability in Action: Air France/KLM: Internal Audit

A series of female-male comparative indicators have been included in the steering of human resources policies and management processes (training, careers, quality of life in the workplace, remuneration ...). These indicators are monitored annually within the framework of an audit carried out with each division to make sure women and men are treated equally.

Source: Air France/KLM (2017, p. 84)

Similar to an external assurance provider, internal auditors can review certain indicators in a sustainability report, determine if the sustainability indicator conforms to certain standards such as Global Reporting Initiative (GRI), or review an entire report for accuracy. Because external assurances are costly, often an organization will start with an internal audit of its report before it engages an external assurance provider. If an organization's internal controls and information systems are well maintained, as evidenced by the internal audit team, the external assurance will be less costly and the likelihood is greater that the assurance provider will not find any major weaknesses.

External Assurances: Third-Party Assurance and Commentaries

This section covers two types of external assurance: those provided by third-party providers and those provided by stakeholders. External assurances are performed by independent third parties who are not employees of the organization. Firms that provide external assurances will typically create a team of specialists with expertise in a variety of areas, such as auditing, engineering, science, and business. Because sustainability topics are multidimensional, the assurance team must have expertise in auditing as well as technical expertise on various aspects of the environment and social dimensions, similar to internal audits. Third-party commentary or stakeholder panels are also used by companies to provide feedback on performance, which is useful both to the organization and to the reader of the report. However, their comments are often not published in the sustainability report.

Third-Party Assurance

The role of external assurances in sustainability reporting can be confusing when compared to the role of audits in financial reporting because there are several different types of reviews performed by professional assurance providers, whereas a financial audit is the most common assurance on the financial statements. Reviews performed by assurance providers on sustainability reporting are either limited or reasonable assurance. They can also be general (on the entire report) or specific (on a few indicators or a certain part of the report). As well, the assurance statements are not standardized like financial audits. Therefore, the reader must review the assurance statement carefully. This section helps to recognize several characteristics that are normally found in third-party reviews/assurances.

The International Standard on Assurance Engagements (IAASB ISAE 3000 Revised 2013, p. 7) defines an assurance engagement for the following purpose:

> *a practitioner is to obtain sufficient appropriate evidence in order to express a conclusion designed to enhance the degree of confidence of the intended users other than the responsible party about the subject matter information …*

What does all that mean?

- "a practitioner" is a person or organization who is an independent assurance provider who has no interest in seeing information presented either favorably or unfavorably but rather is neutral.

- "conclusion designed to enhance the degree of confidence" is usually in the form of a statement (assurance statement) about the accuracy of information and is found in the opinion.
- "subject matter information" can be all or part of a sustainability report, an information system, an environmental management system, or a process.

Therefore, for external assurance an organization engages an independent third party (not an employee of the organization) to perform a review and then to make a statement as to the accuracy of the information provided or the adherence to some standard. The assurance provider (the independent third party) then provides an opinion, along with other information, in an assurance statement. Table 7.2 contains a list of characteristics that are generally provided in assurance statements. Not all assurance statements will contain all characteristics, but the more details that are provided, the greater is the ability to judge the breadth and depth of the review and the quality of the assurance.

Table 7.2 Characteristics of independent assurance statements

Characteristic	Answers the Question(s)
Specific addressee	To whom is the assurance provided?
Name of the assurance provider	Who performed the review?
Extent of the review that was performed	Was it limited or reasonable?
Responsibilities of organization receiving assurance	What does the assurer assume the organization did to prepare the report?
Scope of the review/responsibilities of assurer	Which indicators or operations were assured?
Limitations or exclusions	Were any activities not included?
Procedures used or work performed	What was done during the review?
Standard(s) used to perform the review	Were professional or well-accepted standards followed to ensure a high-quality review?
Standard(s) used to assess the reporting	Did the review determine if the report adheres to a standard or a mix of standards?
Independence of the assurer	How objective is the assurer?

Qualifications of the assurer	Does the assurer have the experience and education to provide the review?
Opinion or conclusions	What decision was made upon completion?
Observations/recommendations for improvement	Were suggestions made for improvement?
Organization's response	Did the organization respond to the observations/recommendations?

Several of these characteristics deserve further attention. The following sections provide additional information on the levels of assurance provided (limited and reasonable), assurance provider and expertise, independence, standards used, and scope.

Limited and reasonable assurance. Most assurance standards offer two levels of assurance:

- Limited assurance, sometimes referred to as "negative" assurance (lower level of assurance), often expressed using phrases such as "nothing came to our attention. . ."
- Reasonable assurance, also referred to as "positive" assurance (higher level of assurance), often expressed using phrases such as "in our opinion, the reported information has been presented fairly…"

The level of assurance provided, whether limited or reasonable, will differ depending on the time and effort required to complete the assurance procedures. A higher level of assurance requires more investigation to check for accuracy of the information and therefore is more costly. The assurance provider checks more documents and conducts more interviews with management and staff to express reasonable rather than limited assurance. (For more information on this topic, see *ISAE 3000 Revised* 2013 or GRI's *The external assurance of sustainability reporting* 2013.) Table 7.3 explains the differences in limited versus reasonable assurances.

Assurance Provider and Expertise. In practice, many different types of organizations perform reviews to provide assurance statements; therefore, not all assurances statements are the same. Most assurances are provided

Table 7.3 External assurance: Limited versus reasonable assurance

Characteristic	Limited Assurance	Reasonable Assurance
Other possible names	Negative Assurance	Positive Assurance
Wording used	"nothing has come to our attention that would cause us to believe the information is not accurate in all material aspects …"	"in our opinion, the reported information has been presented fairly in all material aspects …"
Procedures performed	Identifying areas of risk of misstatement; assessing the data management processes and controls; performing procedures such as interviews and analytic testing sufficient to provide limited assurance.	The same procedures for limited assurance but more thorough and detailed checking of the effectiveness of the related controls to provide reasonable assurance of the reliability of the results.
Scope of use	The entire report, all indicators, or a set of selected indicators.	

by public accounting firms, but all of the following types of organizations can provide assurances:

- public accounting firms;
- certification bodies;
- technical experts; and
- specialist firms.

Because each organization has its preferred method of assurance, a reader must know how to determine the underlying value of the assurance and thus the credibility of the information in the report. Each assurance provider will vary on the following characteristics:

- professional training;
- use of professional guidelines;
- rigor of assurance procedures;
- consistency of service provided.

Table 7.4 provides five well-known companies and the name of the assurance provider for their stand-alone sustainability report.

Table 7.4 Sample of companies and their assurance providers

Company	Assurance Provider
BMW	PwC
Coca-Cola	E&Y
Google	Cameron-Cole
Nestlé	Bureau Veritas
Royal Dutch Shell	LRQA (Lloyd's Register Quality Assurance)

Independence. If a fair and unbiased opinion is to be provided on the reported information, the assurance provider must be objective. Because objectivity is difficult to determine, an organization attempts to select a provider who is independent of the organization being serviced. There are several ways in which an assurance provider's independence can be tainted, but here are three key examples:

- The assuring firm has a financial interest in the reporting organization (e.g., employees of an assuring firm own shares in the reporting organization).
- The assuring firm is heavily dependent on the reporting organization for income (e.g., a major client) and therefore runs the risk of losing the organization as a client if the results are not positive.
- The assuring firm is asked to provide assurance on its own work (e.g., the assurance practitioners implement a data management system and then are asked to provide assurance on the data reported via that system).

Auditing Guidelines/Standards. Several professional bodies now provide guidelines or standards to use when reviewing sustainability reporting. The following have been used recently to provide assurance (with the ISAE guideline as the most used):

- ISAE 3000 published by IAASB (International Auditing and Assurance Standards Board).
- AA1000AS published by AccountAbility.

- AICPA AT-C published by the AICPA (American Institute of Certified Public Accountants).

In addition to these general review standards, professional reviewers will also use specific guidelines that apply to a specific industry or a specific aspect of sustainability (e.g., GHG emissions in the mining industry). Here is a sample of some of the other standards/protocols/principles that have been used to provide assurance engagements recently.

- ISAE 3410—Assurance Engagement on GHG Statements.
- ISO 14064-3 GHG.
- The GHG Protocol.
- Principles of the ICMM (International Council on Mining and Metals).
- Oil and Gas Industry Guidance on Voluntary Sustainability Reporting (IPIECA/API).
- Compendium of GHG Emission Estimation Methodologies for the Oil and Gas Industry by American Petroleum Institute (API).

Scope. Some assurances are general and cover all indicators in addition to the narrative in the report. Other assurances cover only specific indicators or certain aspects of the report. It is essential to read the statement carefully to determine the exact scope of the assurance engagement. The assurance provider and the organization negotiate a contract to determine which services will be provided in the assurance engagement. As the cost of the assurance engagement is dependent on the sophistication of the organization's information systems, often an organization will opt for assuring only those indicators that come from its most developed information systems or that are of most importance to its stakeholders. Therefore, the indicators that are assured may differ from one organization to the next. Some assurance engagements also determine if the report is prepared according to a set of guidelines, such as the GRI Reporting Standards.

Both limited and reasonable assurances can be carried out either on the entire set of reported indicators in a report or on a narrower set of selected indicators. If a narrower set is assured, the organization will provide some indication, such as a list, mark, or star, to clarify the level of assurance for each indicator. Table 7.5 provides examples of the types of assurances (limited or reasonable; general or specific) that appear in a sample of companies' sustainability reports.

Table 7.5 Third-party reviews: Limited and reasonable, general, and specific

Organizations will choose the type of assurance that is most appropriate for their state of reporting or that is required by regulation (e.g., in some jurisdictions, companies are required to have their greenhouse gas emissions reporting assured to a level of limited or reasonable).		
Type of Assurance	**Company Example**	**Assurance Details**
Limited Assurance: General	Kesko, headquartered in Finland, operates an extensive store network in eight countries.	Limited assurance provided on the performance indicators (economic, social, and environmental) disclosed in its Annual Report. The review also included checking the report against the GRI Reporting Standards and the AA1000 AccountAbility Principles.
Limited Assurance: Specific	Vodafone, a multinational telecommunications conglomerate, is headquartered in Berkshire, United Kingdom.	Limited assurance provided on information contained in an appendix in the company's report. Specific indicators assured include gender diversity in employment, energy use, GHG emissions, supplier site assessments, factory workers surveyed, fatalities, lost-time incidents, and employing young adults.
Reasonable Assurance: General	This type of assurance is not common. Unable to find a company that had its entire report verified to a reasonable assurance level.	
Reasonable Assurance: Specific	Exxon Mobil, an international oil and gas company, is headquartered in the United States.	Reasonable assurance provided only on the integrity of its processes for determining material topics and for reporting based on two industry guidelines. The accuracy of data and information reported was not verified.
Both Reasonable and Limited Assurance: Specific	Baxter, an international provider of health care solutions, is headquartered in the United States.	Reasonable assurance provided on product innovation, employee health and safety, GHG emissions, and communities. Limited assurance on procurement and logistics.

Although the popularity of assurance for sustainability reporting is growing, it is still not widespread. Here are a few statistics regarding external assurance.

Sustainability in Action: External Assurance

For a recent sample of the largest publicly traded companies in Europe and North America providing sustainability reports, Braam and Peeters (2018) report the following:

- Less than half of the reports contained external assurance, with assurance more popular in Europe than in North America.
- Large, well-performing companies are more likely to use external assurance.
- Limited is more common than reasonable assurance (less than seven percent used a reasonable level of assurance).

Third-Party Commentaries

External assurance providers are engaged, for the most part, to determine if the quantitative information in the report is reasonably accurate. The assurance provider follows a rigorous, repeatable methodology to reach a conclusion about the accuracy of the reported information and generally does not comment on whether the performance or reporting is satisfactory/unsatisfactory or what improvements to make. Nevertheless, some assurance providers are providing brief observations/recommendations on the performance or the report content in the assurance statement, which is often found at the end of the report.

Both feedback from the assurance provider and from stakeholders help to determine if the organization's performance is in the right place (above average, average, and below average), whereas a review of the indicators by an assurance provider generally only assures the accuracy, with no comment on the level of performance. To gather feedback on performance in a two-way conversation, some organizations engage their stakeholders to make suggestions for improvement both in sustainability performance and reporting. Management at various levels review these suggestions to determine the feasibility of implementing them. There are many considerations regarding assurances for sustainability reporting. It is essential that a reader carefully reviews the report to determine the level of confidence in the information provided.

Outotec uses both stakeholders and its limited assurance engagement to receive feedback on its performance and reporting.

Sustainability in Action: Outotec

Outotec, headquartered in Finland, develops leading technologies and services for natural resource use.
Stakeholders' Feedback: *We have also discussed our sustainability reporting with some investors, and their feedback has been considered when planning the report content. We have also asked our employees for feedback about the report, future themes and topics of interest in sustainability communications, using our internal social media.*
Limited Assurance Engagement Feedback: Although the assurance provider offered several comments on both report content and performance, only part of the commentary is provided here (see the report itself for more detail).   **Performance**   *In general, Outotec has prepared the Sustainability Report 2018 in accordance with GRI Reporting Principles. The report is a balanced, consistent and comprehensive representation of the company operations and performs well in terms of quality requirements set for reporting. In addition, the management approach has been developed in a structural manner enabling better understanding of managing the material topics.*   **Report content**   *The report presents the sustainability context of the company operations. It could be further developed by presenting the company performance in reference to broader sustainability goals and context, e.g., by elaborating the long-term perspective in terms of strategy, risks and goals.*   Source: Outotec (2018, 16, p. 62).

Reflection: Assurances

There are many variables to consider regarding assurance quality of sustainability reports. You are a consultant for a small company that is considering having assurance done on its report. What do you tell the firm?

Key Takeaways

- Assurances can be provided by means of an internal or external review or audit.

- Internal assurances can be classified as internal controls and internal audits and are performed by employees of the organization.
- Common internal controls ensure that personnel are committed and capable at all levels of the organization, including standard operating procedures, employee responsibilities, rigorous information systems, and equal attention to sustainability indicators and financial indicators.
- External assurances can be classified as third-party assurances and stakeholder commentaries and are provided by personnel not employed by the organization.
- Internal assurances tend to be proactive (preventative, risk oriented, and future looking); external assurances tend to be reactive (historical and past looking).
- Assurance of any type helps to improve performance and provide credibility because the provider typically gives constructive feedback on ways to improve.
- Assurances help to give confidence that the report is a reasonably accurate reflection of an organization's activities.
- External assurance providers must be independent of the organization receiving the assurance.
- Assurance teams, whether internal or external, require members from multiple areas of expertise.
- External assurances can be limited (negative) or reasonable (positive). Greater time and effort by the assurance provider distinguishes the two types.
- Reviews that provide assurance can be general in nature (cover the entire report) or specific in nature (covering only selected indicators or other selected information).
- It is necessary to read the assurance statement to determine the scope and other characteristics of the assurance engagement, as assurance statements are not standardized.

We seek to continually improve the audit functions and internal controls of our corporate management. Our aim is to create a management approach that goes beyond compliance and reflects the perspectives of our stakeholders.

—ASICS (2017, p. 7)

CHAPTER 8

What the Future Holds

Main purpose: Review the key points in the model for organizational sustainability and discuss how to continue to improve both performance and reporting in the future.

Objectives: After reading this chapter, you should be able to do the following:

- Recognize the key steps to build a system for organizational sustainability performance and reporting and identify the key questions to ask for each of the steps.
- Comprehend the numerous reporting demands and requests that are placed on organizations, especially companies.
- Grasp that many questions are left unanswered regarding the best approach to provide relevant sustainability reporting to an organization's stakeholders.
- Imagine what the future may bring regarding sustainability performance and reporting.

The best way to predict the future is to create it.
—Peter Drucker

Recapitulation

Let's review what we have learned thus far and discuss the future of sustainability performance and reporting. In Table 8.1 the first column describes the steps an organization would take on its sustainability journey. The second column explains the considerations for accomplishing the step. Each step is followed by an appropriate quotation to illustrate how a company implements the step.

Table 8.1 Major steps in an organization's sustainability system

Develop the Vision, Mission, and Policy Through Stakeholder Engagement	
1. Understand stakeholder perspectives of material aspects for defining the overall policy and measurable objectives for the next year, two to five years, and possibly even ten years.	What do employees feel the organization should achieve? What do primary and secondary external stakeholders expect? What are peers doing? Which multi-stakeholder groups/organizations should the organization join to stay on top of topics important to the sector and broader society? What are the material issues that the organization faces? What can the organization realistically accomplish?
We think about the issues that are of importance to us, that you and I hear about on the news, which is going to dictate what goes into our sustainability report . . . what some of the current issues are from a community perspective, what perspective is emerging from the environmental community. So it's really a constant influence that goes into how to report, and I guess that's going back to the role of the stakeholders. They have an opportunity to influence us at any time, and we as a responsible company need to listen to that and respond as we go along. —Anonymous Reporting Company	
Plan for Action	
2. Identify critical success factors, determine strategy, and implement a management system to accomplish objectives that flow from the policy.	What are the challenges (risks) and opportunities associated with each objective that might affect accomplishing it? Are the board, top management, and all operational units aware of, committed to, and capable of achieving the policy and objectives? What are the strategies, tactics, and operations necessary to accomplish the policy and objectives? Does each employee understand his or her responsibilities for achieving the objectives? How does the organization build commitment and motivation to comply and innovate? Should objectives/goals be part of employees' compensation or recognition? Are the organization's current resources (financial, natural, built, human, and relationship) sufficient to develop capability to achieve the objectives? How are the resources allocated to business units and are their budgets sufficient to start and complete initiatives? What targets should be set?
Sustainability helps us deliver high-quality services, create places where people thrive and minimize our environmental impact. Sustainability also helps us manage risks and opportunities from changing market and societal trends, technology and regulation. This provides value to our fund investors and shareholders. Effective sustainability management requires integration in all parts of our business, from investments and developments to operations and asset management. Our program is overseen by our Executive Sustainability Steering Committee, which sets annual objectives and reports on our progress. —Kevin Adolphe, President and CEO, Manulife Real Estate (2018, p. 4)	

Develop a System to Measure Performance	
3. Determine appropriate indicators to monitor progress. Integrate all indicators into a performance measurement system.	Which indicators flow from the policy commitments and objectives? Which indicators measure progress on material topics? Which indicators are the organization's peers reporting? Which indicators are already reported by law, regulation, financial reporting, or societal pressure? Which indicators have SMART characteristics? Is the system complete and balanced? Does the measurement system include input, output, outcome, and impact indicators if possible? Does the measurement system include efficiency and effectiveness indicators? Will the indicators be assigned to an employee in the organization? If the trend of the indicator moves in the wrong direction, does it require action by an employee? Who will use the information (internal or external) that the indicator provides? If no one, should it be eliminated from the system or should the indicator be assigned to an employee? Are there too many indicators to manage, leaving no time for actual performance improvement?

The biggest measurement challenge we've uncovered in our research is that Dell's major impacts and opportunities are not in the same domain. Our biggest impact comes from the emissions resulting from the energy our customers have to purchase to operate our equipment. We can measure this through carbon footprint calculations. But our opportunities range from enabling microgrids that incorporate more renewables to fighting rare diseases to unlocking underserved children's learning potential. Quantifying the outcomes of these opportunities—or our "handprint"—thus involves many disparate units of measurement—some easily compared, others completely different.

—Dell (2018; pp. 20–21)

Collect the Data	
4. Build an information system to collect the data for calculating indicators.	Which data are the organization already collecting? Are the data in the format needed for calculating the indicators? What new data collection or information systems are needed to collect the data for the indicators? Can the data be collected without undue costs? Can any leading, lagging indicator relationships be developed? Is it possible to develop cross-cutting indicators: eco-efficiency or socioeconomic indicators? Are internal controls incorporated to ensure accuracy of data collection? Are internal audits necessary to check the integrity of the information system?

We use a Maturity Matrix to assess the status of the safety culture in each of our local markets. It assesses progress on the basis of safety leadership, safety learning, employee engagement, supply chain management, governance and assurance, and integrates elements of the International Safety Rating System – a worldwide framework to audit corporate safety performance. It also focuses on the most significant risks in our business with an emphasis on improving performance rather than simply complying with standards.

Vodafone Group Plc (2018, p. 56)

Prepare the Sustainability Report	
5. Communicate progress in a report.	Which reporting frameworks, standards, and guidelines are available? Is the reporting consistent with the material topics, considering the organization's context and stakeholders? Who is the intended audience, and what is the best format and level of technicality to report to each audience/stakeholder? Do different regions require segmented performance results? Is an integrated or stand-alone report most appropriate? What narrative disclosure will help to interpret the results (completeness)? If the indicator is trending in the wrong direction, does the narrative explain management's intentions to change it? Are footnotes provided for additional clarification (clarity)? Are benchmarks provided for context and comparability? Does the reporting contain accomplishments and challenges (balance)? Is the reporting updated frequently (timeliness)? Should an assurance provider check the accuracy of certain indicators? Can a stakeholder panel provide feedback on performance and the reliability of reporting? Do internal decision makers use the results of the report to influence strategic direction?

We made significant progress in setting up our internal systems and training our teams on our new business standards. We are taking steps to establish relevant key performance indicators to continually measure our progress. Access will be a key measure of success for our leaders and employees, and we will be transparent in sharing our successes and our learnings.

—Novartis (2018, p. 19)

Reflect on progress to determine action plans for the next period	
6. Reflect on the sustainability process.	What has the organization learned from its sustainability journey? What are its successes and how can the organization continue to improve? In which areas did it fall short? What lessons did it learn that it can apply going forward? How does the organization's performance compare with its peers?

	How does the organization's performance compare with its stakeholders' needs and desires?
	To what extent has the organization met its obligations under its signed commitments?
	What adjustments are needed going forward?

Performance is very important and we must not lose sight of that in what we do. Sustainability reports are not there to simply communicate a message of the past to our stakeholders, they should also be a signal to our future, that they should drive up performance improvement. We consider a group of twelve North American companies to be our primary peers. So, we look at those along with some others who may not necessarily be our peers but are considered to be leaders in this field of reporting. Internally, which is even more important, we use the report so employees know who we are, and we will keep a copy of this report and give it to a new hire.
—Anonymous Reporting Company

From the review of the steps necessary for an organization to begin its sustainability journey and the related quotations, it is evident that many large companies with recognizable names and brands are committed to integrating environmental and social topics within their business models. Nevertheless, the question arises as to whether all organizations are moving fast enough and pressing hard enough to make the substantial changes that are necessary. For this reason, many institutions (investors, asset managers, trade associations, and NGOs) are getting into the business of pressuring companies to provide sustainability disclosures in their own customized format according to their own guidelines, when that information may already be available in a company document.

A Plethora of Sustainability Reporting

Throughout the chapters of this book we have used the terms "sustainability reporting" or "sustainability information" or "sustainability disclosure." The reason is that companies, especially large multinational corporations that create the most impact, have multiple requests from a variety of organizations for information about their environmental and social performance. Companies prepare a stand-alone sustainability report (or a report that has a slightly different name) or an integrated report that contains information about the progress on economic, environmental, and social activities *along with* the financial *progress*. However, organizations (such as institutional investors, assets managers, environmental organizations, and others) often put forth specialized, customized requests instead of using the company's sustainability report for the needed information. Consequently, companies receive an overwhelming number of surveys to complete when the information, for the most part, is available in its sustainability or integrated report.

Some survey requests ask for detailed disclosure on one aspect, such as the CDP (carbon, forestry, and water). Others want broad-based reporting on every social and environmental topic whether or not material to the specific company. This huge boom in demand for sustainability reporting within the 2010 to 2020 period has put a costly burden on companies. It can create a dilemma for the company as to how to respond in a responsible manner to the numerous demands for information in a customized, one-off questionnaire when the company has already invested substantially to provide the information in an integrated or stand-alone sustainability report. When companies do not respond to customized requests for information but rather suggest the information can be found in its sustainability report, the company can sometimes be labeled as "irresponsible" by the requesting institution. This concern is illustrated with a quotation by a company that has reported for 30 years and is truly committed to the process.

Sustainability in Action: Commentary on Request for Sustainability Information

Too many ... too many requests. They all have very good justification and each one is different, and if we were to prepare documentation to fit all of those requests especially from every investor and investor analyst, we'll probably have twelve people working full time on that, it's very intensive. It is intensive because every request is different. We've been doing reporting for over 30 years but, we have to slice and dice each survey request in a different way. Now, don't get me wrong. The principle of open reporting is right in my heart. It is absolute that we must do it. My problem is trying to recognize the different reporting requirements and requests for all these organizations. The various users of sustainability reports need to talk together. They need to collaborate with one another far more than they are doing right now. And that has got to carry on big time, and so much that there's got to be more convergence instead of divergence.

—Anonymous Energy Reporting Company

Websites: Sources of Reports and Reporting

To address numerous information requests, large proactive multinational companies attempt to predict what information stakeholders will request to avoid addressing individual requests. Iberdrola is a multinational electrics company headquartered in Spain and has the reports available on its website, as detailed in Table 8.2.

Table 8.2 Iberdrola's reporting

Annual Report	Guideline or Standard
Integrated Report	International Integrated Reporting Council (IIRC)
Financial Report	International Financial Reporting Standards (IFRS)
Annual Corporate Governance Report	National Securities Market Commission of Spain
Sustainability Report	Global Reporting Initiative (GRI with external assurance)
Activities Report of the B of D and Committees	Iberdrola internal standards
Director Remuneration Report	National Securities Market Commission of Spain
Related-Party Transactions with Directors and Significant Shareholders	Iberdrola internal standards
Shareholder Engagement Report	Iberdrola internal standards
Independence of the Auditor	Iberdrola internal standards
Other Reports	
Quarterly Results	
UBE Watch Fact Sheet	
Quarterly Shareholder Bulletin	
Innovation Report	
Corporate Environmental Footprint	
Biodiversity	
Greenhouse Gas Report	
Iberdrola, Integrated Report, Reporting Overview, p. 4	

Likely there are other reports that could be added to the list. In addition to the primary sustainability or integrated report, industry associations (especially in the extractive industries, such as energy, chemical, mining, and foresty) must adhere to reporting guidelines requested by their industry associations. The Securities Exchange Commission (SEC) in the United States, as well as other securities commissions, request reporting on the use of conflict minerals and CEO pay ratio to the average worker salary. Even the standard setters creating the guidelines are questioning if there are too many requests placed on companies that are not harmonized; consequently, the Corporate Reporting Dialogue was recently created (discussed in Chapter 2). We need to work together to find ways that companies can provide useful, relevant information to its stakeholders that is cost beneficial.

Organizations must work with their stakeholders to be alert to evolving perspectives and integrate those perspectives to keep policies and management systems current. Consequently, they will be well positioned to serve a higher purpose than just creating financial returns for their stakeholders. We will all be working together to create organizations that are solving society's problems.

Reflection: Cost Benefit of Reporting

For financial accounting the cost-benefit principle helps to determine if additional disclosure is necessary internally as well as externally. Generally, the cost of preparation of the financial information should not exceed the benefit received from the additional disclosure. Does this principle also apply to sustainability reporting and are companies to the limit where the cost has exceeded the internal and external benefit to stakeholders? If not, why not? If so, how can the situation be improved?

The Future of Sustainability Reporting

Professional organizations with interest in corporate reporting are attempting to find answers to many unanswered questions. As we move forward to improve the sustainability reporting process, we must find ways to provide relevant credible information in an efficient and effective manner for the reporting organization and its stakeholders. A few of the questions that were raised in the previous chapters are provided here.

- Does our current capitalistic economic system need adjustments to be able to address the environmental and social problems that society is facing?
- If sustainability disclosure is integrated in the annual financial report, are the informational needs of nonfinancial stakeholders being marginalized by not having a separate, easy-to-read sustainability report for them?
- Is it better if institutions that develop reporting guidelines (e.g., the SASB approach) determine which topics are material for each industry/sector or should determining materiality be left up to the reporting organization by engaging with its stakeholders (e.g., the GRI approach)?
- Are there benefits of engaging with stakeholders other than to determine materiality topics?
- What are the pros and cons of mandatory versus voluntary reporting?
- How can organizations address the many specialized requests for sustainability information in a more efficient and effective manner?
- When sustainability disclosure cross cuts with financial reporting disclosure, is providing links or notations to other company documents (where the disclosure can be found) an effective manner to lessen the cost of preparing separate documents?

Can you add questions to this list that will be important in the future of sustainability reporting?

What will be your role in finding answers to these questions?

Through our core business, we help prevent and treat diseases, ease suffering and improve quality of life for people worldwide. However, as the size and complexity of the world's healthcare challenges grow, we must widen our scope and extend our impact even further. It begins with a fundamental shift in the way we do business – with the clear intention of bridging the divide between those with access to critical healthcare innovations, and those without.

—Novartis in Society (2018, p. 19)

Glossary

Accountability: An obligation to account for one's responsibilities, often accomplished through some form of reporting process to answer for one's actions.

Accurate: A description of information or indicators that are free of errors and that fairly represent the activities of an organization.

Achievable: A description of an activity, indicator, or target that can be accomplished. To be achievable, the item should be linked to someone's responsibilities and thus require action.

Assurance: A provision of confidence or certainty given by an independent assurance provider to certain subject matter.

Assurance engagement: An agreement whereby the organization contracts an assurance provider to express an opinion about the reliability of some aspect of an organization's activities; also called assurance service.

Assurance statement: A short report providing an opinion about the credibility of the subject matter, often information in a sustainability report regarding an organization's activities.

Balance: Reporting both accomplishments and challenges; providing information on both positive and negative activities.

Benchmark: A point of reference or standard used to place performance in context.

Board of directors: The governing body of a corporation or organization, elected by its shareholders (owners) or membership, to provide direction to the managers who should act in the best interest of its owners, members, or donors.

Brundtland Report: An outcome of the WCED that defined sustainable development with an economic, environmental, and social component. Its main message is that nations need to work together for "*development that meets the needs of the present without compromising the ability of future generations to meet their own needs.*" Also known as *Our Common Future*.

Capitalism: An economic system in which most of the means of production are owned by private enterprises, rather than by the government, with the purpose of making profits.

CDP: Formerly the Carbon Disclosure Project, the CDP manages a disclosure system on carbon, forestry, and water. Most respondents are corporations, but some government bodies and other organizations also respond to its annual questionnaires.

CERES: The Coalition for Environmentally Responsible Economies is a group of environmental, investor, and advocacy organizations coordinating efforts to promote sustainable practices. CERES brought forth the Valdez Principles and was instrumental in initiating the Global Reporting Institute (GRI).

CDSB: The Climate Disclosure Standards Board's objective is to provide a framework for reporting natural capital that is as rigorous as financial capital reporting.

Certain subject matter: The processes and procedures incorporated in an information system or an environmental or social management system, which is the subject of an assurance. Examples are the accuracy of certain indicators, the accuracy of accounting for greenhouse gas (GHG) emissions, or the adherence to a certain standard.

Comparable: The ability to judge an organization's performance against others. Benchmarks are beneficial for comparability purposes.

Complete: A description of information that includes all material activities, provides balance, and compares performance to other organizations, year-to-year, or to a standard.

Conflict minerals: Natural resources mined in an area of human conflict, with the revenues used to support the conflict.

Control system: All of the integrated processes and procedures that an organization has implemented to achieve an objective. A control system is part of a management system that includes both planning and control.

Corporate Reporting Dialogue: An initiative convened by the IIRC that attempts to harmonize reporting frameworks, standards, and requirements for both financial and sustainability reporting, consisting of the CDP, CDSB, GRI ISO, SASB, IFRS. FASB is an observer.

Cost effective: A description of an activity that can be achieved with the least cost, thus combining effectiveness and efficiency.

CSR: Corporate social responsibility or reporting, frequently used instead of sustainability. CSR defines how corporations should act but is less clearly defined than sustainability.

Decision making: Logical thought processes that stakeholders, as well as stockholders, use to gather information to take action in the future.

Eco-efficiency: Activities or indicators that integrate both economic and environmental objectives. Indicators of eco-efficiency have one dimension related to the environment and the other related to the economy (one is the numerator and the other the denominator).

Economic: A dimension of sustainability that represents the production, manufacture, and distribution (along with other activities) of economic goods and services.

Effectiveness indicator: A metric which determines if an objective is met, regardless of cost, such as ratings for employee satisfaction.

GLOSSARY

Efficiency indicator: A metric which measures output related to input. Products or services produced (output) are divided by resources used to produce them (input), such as emissions per barrel of oil produced.

Environment: A dimension of sustainability that represents a system of maintaining integrity of the ecosystems to enable them to continue to produce and function for future generations.

Environmental reporting: A means of providing information about an organization's environmental performance, similar to sustainability reporting; however, the focus is only on one of the three dimensions of sustainability: the environmental dimension.

ESG: A term used to refer to environmental, social, and governance performance. Governance is partially substituted for the economic dimension of sustainability.

External assurance: A statement by an independent third party about the accuracy of information and/or adequacy of performance. It involves the engagement of a qualified person outside of the organization to comment on, and provide opinions about, performance or reporting.

GHG emissions: Greenhouse gases, such as carbon dioxide and methane, that appear to be causing climate change.

Greenwashing: Performance or reporting that appears environmentally responsible on the surface but further investigation suggests that it is actually superficial, not showing depth.

GRI: The Global Reporting Initiative, an international organization that has prepared guidelines, and most recently standards, with the support of a multidisciplinary group of stakeholders. Organizations use the standards to prepare their sustainability reports.

GRI Sector Disclosures: A supplemental guideline or standard, which is customized by the Global Reporting Initiative for a certain industry.

Guideline: A source of reference for principles or rules on a certain topic.

IIRC: International Integrated Reporting Council, an organization which comprises regulators, investors, companies, standard setters, the accounting profession, and non-government organizations (NGOs) that work to establish integrated reporting as the mainstream format for sustainability reporting.

ISO: International Organization for Standardization, an organization that brings together standard setting organizations in 160 countries to develop and publish international standards that meet the needs both of business and broader society.

Independent assurance provider: A firm or person who is not biased in his/her opinion regarding information provided by the organization and has no interest in seeing information presented either favorably or unfavorably.

Indicator: A means of quantification using a metric. Even though performance can be presented in qualitative, narrative form, organizations and stakeholders usually prefer quantitative indicators to easily and quickly assess trends, challenges, and accomplishments.

Input: An activity or indicator which measures what is going into a process, such as dollars invested into a community, but it does not determine what result occurred with those dollars.

Integrated Report or Reporting: A principles-based framework, promoted by the IIRC, that focuses on how a company creates value over a short-, medium-, and long-term period through the maintenance of six capitals.

Internal assurance: Internal controls and internal audits are two forms of internal assurance that are carried out by employees of the reporting organization to monitor operating results, verify records, and assist with increasing efficiency and effectiveness of operations.

Internal audit: Frequent reviews to evaluate internal controls, monitor operating results, and verify records to increase the efficiency and effectiveness of operations and to detect fraud.

Internal audit department (function): A unit within an organization that consists of internal auditors who perform ongoing audits or reviews at a more detailed level than that of an external assurance provider.

Internal auditor: An employee who provides unbiased consultation on internal controls through audit and assurance services. Internal auditors should report to the highest level of management and the board of directors to ensure independence.

Internal controls: Procedures and practices that direct, motivate, or deter certain types of behavior to help meet an organization's objectives.

Lagging Indicators: Detective measures or metrics used after an activity occurs.

Leading Indicators: Preventive measures or metrics used before an activity occurs.

Legitimate: A description given to an organization that is producing a good or service in a manner that stakeholders and society wish. Related to legitimacy theory.

Limited assurance: The result of a review or audit having a narrower scope and less depth than reasonable assurance or a full audit, usually confined to certain accounts or operations; sometimes called negative assurance.

MD&A: The Management Discussion and Analysis section of a company's annual report in which management explains numerous aspects of the company's financial performance, both past and present, occasionally the future.

MDGs: The eight Millennium Development Goals of the United Nations Member States which are the predecessors to the SDGs. They were the first formal call to action with specific targets for all entities to operate more sustainably with an achievement date of 2015.

Material: Information that is important to a decision.

Materiality matrix: A means of classifying sustainability topics to the extent of their "importance to stakeholders" and "impact on the organization," often found in the sustainability report. The Global Reporting Institute (GRI) requests this approach to linking stakeholders' needs and desires to a company's sustainability activities and reporting.

Measurable: An activity or indicator which can be put in the form of numbers or metrics.

Multi-stakeholder process: A course of action that includes opinions and expertise from a variety of organizations, groups, or individuals that have an interest in, or are affected by, the result.

Nested circles: A means of illustrating the concept of sustainability in which the economic dimension is nested within the social dimension, which in turn is nested within the environmental dimension.

Objective: An aim, goal, or intention. Objectives are the most basic planning tools underlying all strategic activities.

Outcome: An activity or indicator which measures the result of the input or output (such as health effects or satisfaction from eating the meals).

Output: An activity or indicator which measures what is coming out of a process (such as number of food bank meals provided).

PERI: The Public Environmental Reporting Initiative, one of the first guidelines to help organizations communicate environmental performance information to its stakeholders.

Performance: An action that helps to accomplish an objective or goal. It is usually measured in the form of metrics/indicators such as pre-determined standards of completeness, cost, or speed.

Performance measurement system: A complete set of indictors consisting of metrics used to quantify how well an organization fulfilled its responsibilities as identified in its policy.

Primary stakeholder: A person, group or organization that transacts with a company, such as customers, employees, suppliers, shareholders, and financial institutions. Also, stakeholders that are included in a company's product life cycle or value added chain.

Reasonable assurance: A review or audit having a broader scope and more depth than undertaken for limited assurance; also called positive assurance. However, no audit or review can provide absolute certainty that an event will (or will not) occur or that data are absolutely accurate.

Regulator: Part of a system which determines and maintains the operating parameters usually within specified limits or scopes. A regulator may be an electronic or mechanical device or a person which ensures certain actions are (or are not) undertaken.

Relevant: Information, topics, or indicators that are significant, important, and useful for making decisions. They also reflect the core values and strategy of the company and the expectations of the stakeholders.

Reporting organization: A business organization, non-profit organization, government, or non-government organization that provides information in a report form on some aspect of its environmental, social, and economic performance. The report provided is generally referred to as a sustainability or a corporate social responsibility (CSR) report.

Risk strategy: Plans, policies, procedures, and controls used to minimize the probability of a negative event occurring.

SASB: The Sustainability Accounting Standards Board, an organization established to develop standards for reporting of material sustainability topics (in securities commissions' filings) for publicly-held companies. Material topics differ among industries.

SDGs: The 17 Sustainable Development Goals were adopted by the United Nations Member States to call all entities to operate in a more sustainable manner with a targeted achievement date of 2030.

SMART: An acronym used for the following characteristics of indicators or targets: Specific, Measurable, Achievable, Relevant, and Timely.

Secondary stakeholder: A person, group or organization that is affected by, or can affect, the transactions and activities of a company, such as community groups, non-government organizations, governments, human rights advocates, and environmental advocates.

Shareholder: Any person, company or other institution that owns at least one share of stock in a company. Shareholders are the owners of a company. They have the potential to profit or lose depending on the company's financial operations; also referred to as stockholders.

Specific: A description for an indicator that is valid and credible. It is clean and simple, easy to interpret, comparable with others, and understandable.

Spin: Presentation of a situation or information in a biased or slanted manner, not balanced or complete.

Social: One of the dimensions of sustainability represents a system of living in groups or communities rather than in isolation.

Social license: A theoretical concept suggesting that an organization (primarily a business) can operate if it provides value in the form that society desires.

Stakeholder engagement: Contact with an organization's stakeholders to exchange ideas.

Sustainability: The ability to maintain a state in which the economy, environmental resources, and social needs and wants are harmonized to ensure resilience of the planet and a high quality of life for future generations.

Sustainable capitalism: A form of economic system in which the primary means of production are held by private enterprises but considers the carrying capacity of the planet and the needs and expectations of all stakeholders.

TFCD: Task Force on Climate-related Financial Disclosures, an organization established to develop the necessary risk disclosures related to the climate.

Timely: A description for an indicator that is collected when data are needed to warn if corrective action is necessary and is available to stakeholders when needed for their decision making.

Transparent: An action, method, procedure or information which lacks hidden agendas and conditions.

Unbiased party: An individual without an interest in the organization and therefore would have no motive for an assessment to be positive or negative.

Venn diagram: A means of illustrating the concept of sustainability in which circles representing the three concepts of sustainability (economic, social, and environment) partially overlap each other.

WCED: World Commission on Environment and Development, created to address growing concern about the accelerating deterioration of the human condition and natural resources and the consequences of that deterioration for economic and social development. The WCED published the Brundtland Report in 1987. Also called our *Common Future*, which brought forth the concept of sustainable development.

References

Account Ability. 2015. *AA1000SES Stakeholder Engagement Standard.* https://accountability.org/wp-content/uploads/2016/10/AA1000SES_2015.pdf (accessed 2015).

Adolphe, Kevin President and CEO. "2018. Manulife Real Estate Embedding Sustainability In Our Business." *2018 Real Estate Sustainability Report.* https://manuliferealestate.com/sites/default/files/downloads/sustainability-report-2018.pdf (accessed 2018).

Air France KLM. 2017. *Corporate Social Responsibility Report.* CSR Strategy. https://csrreport2017.airfranceklm.com/ (accessed 2017).

Alma Media. 2018. *Corporate Responsibility Report.* GRI Index. https://almamedia.fi/docs/default-source/investors/financial-reporting/en/2018/alma_vastuuullisuus2018_eng_final.pdf?sfvrsn=9914e7ed_4 (accessed 2018).

Apple. *2018 Progress Report. Covering fiscal Year 2017.* https://apple.com/environment/pdf/Apple_Environmental_Responsibility_Report_2018.pdf (accessed 2017).

ASICS. 2017. *I Move Me. Sustainability Report.* https://assets.asics.com/page_types/3734/files/asics_sustainability_report_2017_online_original.pdf?1528664869 (accessed 2017).

BHP. 2018. Sustainability Report. https://bhp.com/-/media/documents/investors/annual-reports/2018/bhpsustainabilityreport2018.pdf

Bank of America. 2017. *Environmental, Social & Governance Performance Data Summary.* https://about.bankofamerica.com/assets/pdf/Bank-of-America-2017-ESG-Performance-Data-Summary.pdf (accessed 2017).

Baxter. 2017. *Corporate Responsibility Report. Making a Meaningful Difference.* https://baxter.com/sites/g/files/ebysai746/files/2018-06/Baxter_2017_Corporate_Responsibility_Report%20_0.pdf) (accessed 2017).

Beinhocker, E., and N. Hanauer. September, 2014. "Redefining Capitalism." *McKinsey Quarterly.* https://mckinsey.com/featured-insights/long-term-capitalism/redefining-capitalism (accessed September, 2014).

Bowen, F., A. Newenham-Kahindi, and I. Herremans. 2010. "When Suits Meet Roots: The Antecedents and Consequences of Community Engagement Strategy." *Journal of Business Ethics* 95, pp. 297–318.

Braam, Geert and Peeters, Roy. 2018. "Corporate Sustainability Performance and Assurance on Sustainability Reports: Diffusion of Accounting Practices in the Real of Sustainable Development." *Corporate Social Responsibility and Environmental Management* 25, pp. 164–81.

REFERENCES

Brundtland, Gro Harlem and World Commission on Environment and Development. 1987. *Our Common Future*. Oxford: Oxford University Press.

Business Roundtable (BR). August 19, 2019. "Business Roundtable Redefines the Purpose of A Corporation to Promote 'An Economy that Serves All Americans.'" https://businessroundtable.org/business-roundtable-redefines-the-purpose-of-a-corporation-to-promote-an-economy-that-serves-all-americans (accessed August 19, 2019).

CDP (formerly the Carbon Disclosure Project) n.d. at: https://cdp.net/en (accessed June 15, 2019).

Canadian Institute of Chartered Accountants (CICA) n.d. *Criteria of Control* (CoCo). http://cica.ca/cica/cicawebsite.nsf/public/SGControlRiskGovernance (accessed May 20, 2019).

Canon. 2019. *Sustainability Report 2019: An Integrated Report for a Better World*. https://global.canon/en/csr/report/pdf/canon-sus-2019-e.pdf (accessed 2019).

Carbon Disclosure Standards Board (CDSB) n.d. at: https://cdsb.net/ (accessed June 15, 2019).

Carson, Rachael. 1962. *Silent Spring*. Boston: Houghton Mifflin.

Centre for Sustainability and Excellence (CSE). 2017. Sustainability Reporting Trends in North America, https://cse-net.org/wp-content/uploads/documents/Sustainability-Reporting-Trends-in-North%20America%20_RS.pdf (accessed 2017).

Ceres. n.d. https://ceres.org (accessed June 10, 2019).

Certified B Corporation. n.d. FAQ Items. *What's the difference between a Certified B Corp and a benefit corporation?* https://bcorporation.net/faq-item/whats-difference-between-certified-b-corp-and-corporation (accessed May 20, 2019).

Committee of Sponsoring Organizations (COSO) of the Treadway Commission and World Business Council for Sustainable Development (WBCSD). October 2018. *Enterprise Risk Management: Applying Enterprise Risk Management to Environmental, Social and Governance-Related Risks* (accessed October 2018).

ConocoPhillips. 2017. *Sustainability Report*. http://static.conocophillips.com/files/resources/18-0231-2017-sustainable-report.pdf (accessed 2017).

Dell. 2018. *FY18 Dell's Legacy of Good Annual Update on Progress*. https://delltechnologies.com/content/dam/delltechnologies/assets/microsites/legacyofgood/2018/pdf/Dell-FY18%20Legacy%20of%20Good%20Annual%20Update.pdf (accessed 2018).

DeSimone, Livio D. and Frank Popoff with the World Business Council for Sustainable Development (WBCSD). 2000. *Eco-efficiency: The Business Link to Sustainable Development*. Massachusetts, Cambridge and England, London: The MIT Press.

DiCaprio, Tamara. December 2013. "The Microsoft Carbon Fee: Theory & Practice. The What, Why, and How of Microsoft's Efforts to Drive Culture Change. Microsoft." https://microsoft.com/en-us/search?q=DiCaprio%2C+Tamara.+2013%2C+December.+The+Microsoft+Carbon+-Fee%3A++Theory+%26+Practice.+The+What%2C+Why%2C+and+How+of+Microsoft%E2%80%99s+Efforts+to+Drive+Culture+Change.+Microsoft (accessed December 2013).

Domtar Corporation. 2017. *Sustainability Report.* Efficient Manufacturing, Water A Shared Resource. https://domtar.com/sites/default/files/2017-12/PDF/Domtar_SGR2017_ENG.pdf (accessed 2017).

Dow Jones Sustainability Index (DJSI). 2019. https://robecosam.com/csa/indices/?r (accessed March 10, 2019).

Dowling, John and Pfeffer, Jeffrey. 1975. Organizational Legitimacy: Social Values and Organizational Behaviors. The Pacific Sociological Review 18(1) 122–136.

Edelman. 2019. *Edelman Trust Barometer Global Report.* https://edelman.com/trust-barometer (accessed 2019).

ExxonMobil. 2017. Sustainability Report. LRQA Independent Assurance Statement. https://corporate.exxonmobil.com/en/community-engagement/sustainability-report/lrqa-independent-assurance-statement (accessed 2017).

Financial Accounting Standards Board (FASB). September, 2010. "Chapter 3, Qualitative Characteristics of Useful Financial Information." In *Conceptual Framework for Financial Reporting. Statement of Financial Accounting Concepts No. 8,* 16–22. Financial Accounting Foundation.

Forum for the Future. n.d. "The Five Capitals Model." https://forumforthefuture.org/the-five-capitals (accessed May 15, 2019).

Ford. 2017/2018. *Sustainability Report.* Letter from William Clay Ford, Jr. (Executive Chairman) and Jim Hackett (President and Chief Executive Officer) https://corporate.ford.com/content/dam/corporate/en/company/2017-18-Sustainability-Report/sr17.pdf (accessed 2017/2018).

Freeman, E. 1984. *Strategic Management: A Stakeholder Approach.* Boston: Pitman.

Global Reporting Initiative (GRI). 2018. *Consolidated Set of Global Reporting Initiative Reporting Standards.* Stichting Global Reporting Initiative.

Global Reporting Initiative (GRI). 2016. *G4 Sector Disclosures.* https://globalreporting.org/information/sector-guidance/Pages/default.aspx (accessed 2016).

Global Reporting Initiative (GRI). 2013. Research & Development Series. *The External Assurance of Sustainability Reporting.* Stichting Global Reporting Initiative.

Google. 2018. *Environmental Report.* Progress Against Targets. https://storage.googleapis.com/gweb-sustainability.appspot.com/pdf/Google_2018-Environmental-Report.pdf (accessed 2018).

REFERENCES

Hewlett Packard. 2017. HPE Living Progress Report. https://assets.ext.hpe.com/is/content/hpedam/documents/a00048000-8999/a00048490/a00048490enw.pdf (accessed 2017).

Iberdrola. 2019. Shareholders and Investors. *Annual Report.* https://iberdrola.com/shareholders-investors/annual-reports (accessed 2019).

Institute of Internal Auditors (IIIA) n.d. *Value of Internal Auditing: Assurance, Insight, Objectivity.* A Presentation to Stakeholders about the Value of Internal Auditing and Related PowerPoint Presentation. https://na.theiia.org/about-ia/PublicDocuments/PR-Value_Prop_Bro-FNL-Lo.pdf (accessed May 12, 2019).

Institute of Internal Auditors (IIA) Australia. 2018. *Factsheet: Internal Audit versus External Audit.* http://iia.org.au/sf_docs/default-source/technical-resources/2018-fact-sheets/internal-audit-versus-external-audit.pdf?sfvrsn=2 (accessed 2018).

Intel. 2017–2018. *Corporate Responsibility Report* https://integratedreporting.org/wp-content/uploads/2013/03/IR-Background-Paper-Capitals.pdf (accessed 2017–2018).

International Accounting Standards Board (IASB). September, 2010. *The Conceptual Framework for Financial Reporting.* IFRS Foundation.

International Auditing and Assurance Standards Board (IAASB). December, 2013. *ISAE 3000 (Revised), Assurance Engagements Other than Audits or Reviews of Historical Financial Information. International Framework for Assurance Engagements and Related Conforming Amendments. Final Pronouncement.* International Federation of Accountants (IFAC).

International Council of Chemical Associations (ICCA). 2019. "Responsible Care." https://icca-chem.org/responsible-care/ (accessed 2019).

International Integrated Reporting Council (IIRC). 2019. "Corporate Reporting Dialogue." *Landscape Map.* International Integrated Reporting Council (IIRC). https://corporatereportingdialogue.com/landscape-map/ (accessed 2019).

International Integrated Reporting Council (IIRC). December, 2013. "The International <IR> Framework." Integrated Reporting. http://integratedreporting.org/wp-content/uploads/2015/03/13-12-08-THE-INTERNATIONAL-IR-FRAMEWORK-2-1.pdf (accessed December, 2013).

International Integrated Reporting Council (IIRC) with ACCA and NBA. March, 2013. *Capitals Background Paper for <IR>.* https://integratedreporting.org/wp-content/uploads/2013/03/IR-Background-Paper-Capitals.pdf (accessed March, 2013).

International Organization for Standardization (ISO) ISO 14000 Series. *ISO 14001 2015. Environmental Management.* https://iso.org/iso-14001-environmental-management.html (accessed 2015).

Johnson Matthey. 2018. *Annual Report and Accounts.* Inspiring Science, Enhancing Life. https://matthey.com/-/media/files/investors/reports/annual-report-2018/annual-report-2018.pdf (accessed 2018).

Kaya, U. and Yayla, H. E. 2007. "Remembering Thirty-five Years of Social Accounting: A Review of the Literature and the Practice." *Munich Personal RePEc Archive (MPRA)* Paper No. 3454, https://mpra.ub.uni-muenchen.de/3454/1/MPRA_paper_3454.pdf (accessed June 9, 2007).

Kesko. 2018. *Kesko's Annual Report 2018 Sustainability.* Independent Practitioner's Assurance Report. https://kesko.fi/globalassets/pdf-tiedostot/kesko_vsk_2018_en-1.pdf (accessed 2018).

Kluckhohn, F.R., and F.L. Strodtbeck. 1961. *Variations in Value Orientations.* Oxford, England: Row, Peterson.

Koch, F. 1979. *The New Corporate Philanthropy: How Society and Business Can Profit.* New York, NY: Plenum Press.

Marks & Spencer (M & S). 2018. *Transformation Underway, Plan A Report.* Health & Safety, p. 15. https://corporate.marksandspencer.com/annual-report-2018/mands_plan_a_2018.pdf (accessed 2018).

Marriott International. 2018. *Serve 360 Report. Sustainability and Social Impact at Marriott International.* http://serve360.marriott.com/wp content/uploads/2018/10/2018_Serve_360_Report.pdf (accessed 2018).

McDonald's Corporation. 2018. *Notice of Annual Shareholders' Meeting and Proxy Statement.* Proxy Statement Pursuant to Section 14(a) of the Securities Exchange Act of 1934. Shareholder Proposals. Proposal 5, pp. 72–73.

Milne, M.J. 1996. "On Sustainability; The Environment and Management Accounting." *Management Accounting Research* 7, pp. 135–61.

Morsing, M., and M. Schultz. 2006. "Corporate Social Responsibility Communication: Stakeholder Information, Response and Involvement Strategies." *Business Ethics: A European Review* 15, no. 4, pp. 323–38.

Nike Inc. 2016/2017. *Sustainable Business Report FY 16/17,* Maximum Performance Minimum Impact. Data Integrity. https://s1.q4cdn.com/806093406/files/doc_downloads/2018/SBR-Final-FY16-17.pdf

Nike Inc. 2018 FY18 Impact Report, Purpose Moves Us, Global Reporting (GRI) Index. https://s3-us-west-2.amazonaws.com/purpose-cms-production01/wp-content/uploads/2019/05/20194957/FY18_Nike_Impact_Report_Final.pdf (accessed 2018).

Novartis. 2018. *Novartis in Society 2018.* p. 19. https://novartis.com/sites/www.novartis.com/files/novartis-in-society-report-2018.pdf (accessed 2018).

Organization of Economic Cooperation and Development (OECD). Guidelines for Multinational Enterprises. 2011 Edition. http://oecd.org/daf/inv/mne/48004323.pdf (accessed 2011).

Outotec. 2018. *Sustainability Report.* https://outotec.com/globalassets/sustainability-report/2018/outotec_sr_2018.pdf (accessed 2018).

Porritt, J. 2007. *Capitalism as If the World Matters*. London; Sterling, VA: Earthscan, 2007. Print.

Porter, M.E., and M.R. Kramer. January-February, 2011. "Creating Shared Value. How to Reinvent Capitalism—and Unleash a Wave of Innovation and Growth." *Harvard Business Review*, pp. 1–17.

Principles of Responsible Investing (PRI). n.d. *What are the Six Principles for Responsible Investment?* https://unpri.org/pri/about-the-pri (accessed May 5, 2019).

Sadler, B. 1990. "Sustainable Development and Water Resource Management." *Alternatives* 17, no. 3, p. 22.

Samsung Electronics. 2018. *Sustainability Report. Inspire the World Create the Future*. Key Stakeholder Engagement and Stakeholder Communication. https://samsung.com/us/smg/content/dam/samsung/us/aboutsamsung/2017/Sustainability_Report_2018_v2.pdf (accessed 2018).

Schneider Electric. 2018. *Schneider Sustainability Impact 2018-2020*. Non-financial results Q1 2019 https://schneider-electric.com/ww/en/documents/Sustainability/2019/04/18-presentation-schneider-sustainability-impact-first-quarter-2019-tcm50-474125.pdf (accessed 2018).

Senge, P.M. 2008. *The Necessary Revolution: How Individuals and Organizations Are Working Together to Create a Sustainable World*. New York, NY: Doubleday.

Starbucks. 2017. *Performance Report. Global Social Impact*. https://starbucks.com/responsibility/global-report (accessed 2017).

Suncor Energy Inc. 2018. Report on Sustainability, Recordable Injury Frequency. https://sustainability.suncor.com/en/downloads (accessed 2018).

SustainAbility. 2019, February. *Rate the Raters 2019: Expert Views on ESG Ratings*. http://sustainability.com/wp-content/uploads/2019/02/sustainability-rate-the-raters-2019.pdf (accessed 2019).

Sustainability Accounting Standards Board (SASB). 2019. https://sasb.org/ (accessed April 27, 2019).

Task Force on Climate Related Financial Disclosure (TCFD) n.d. https://fsb-tcfd.org/ (accessed April 27, 2019).

Teck. 2017. *Horizons. 2017 Sustainability Report*. https://teck.com/media/Teck-2017-Sustainability-Report.pdf (accessed 2017).

Unilever. 2018. *Sustainable Living Report Hub*. https://unilever.com/sustainable-living/our-sustainable-living-report-hub/index.html (accessed 2018).

United National Global Compact-Accenture Strategy CEO Study. 2018. *Special Edition: Transforming Partnerships for the SDGs*.

United Nations. 2015. *Millennium Development Goals and Beyond*. Home. https://un.org/millenniumgoals/ (accessed 2015).

United Nations. 2019. Sustainable Development Goals. Knowledge Platform. Home. https://sustainabledevelopment.un.org/ (accessed 2019).

United Nations SDG Guide. December 14, 2015, Chapter 1: Getting to Know the Sustainable Development Goals. An Introduction to the SDGs. https://sdg.guide/chapter-1-getting-to-know-the-sustainable-development-goals-e05b9d17801 (accessed December 14, 2015).

United Nations Sustainable Development. 1992. United Nations Conference on Environment & Development Rio de Janerio, Brazil 3 to 14, June 1992. Agenda 21. pp. 1–351. https://sustainabledevelopment.un.org/content/documents/Agenda21.pdf (accessed June 14, 1992).

van Houten, Frans. 2014. Philips. *Circular Economy Rethinking the Future. Our Transition Towards a Circular Economy.* Koninklijke Philips N.V. (Royal Philips). philips.com/circulareconomy (accessed 2014).

Vodafone Group Plc. 2018. Sustainable Business Report. https://vodafone.com/content/dam/vodafone-images/sustainability/downloads/sustainablebusiness2018.pdf (accessed 2018).

Warren, R. 2012. *The Purpose Driven Life: What on Earth Am I Here For?* Zondervan.

Wells Fargo & Company. 2019. *Social Responsibility Report. Living Our Commitment.* Corporate Responsibility Committee Charter, https://www08.wellsfargomedia.com/assets/pdf/about/corporate/corporate-responsibility-committee-charter.pdf (accessed 2019).

Zenisek, T.J. 1979. "Corporate Social Responsibility: A Conceptualization Based on Organizational Literature." *The Academy of Management Review* 4, no. 3, pp. 359–368.

About the Author

Dr. Irene M. Herremans has taught sustainability for the past 20 years. She has engaged learners in both formal education at universities and informal education for professionals through seminars, workshops, conferences, and other types of speaking engagements. She has supported sustainability education in several countries throughout the world, including Canada, the United States, Ecuador, Peru, and China to name a few. She has supervised numerous graduate projects and theses on the topic of sustainability. Irene also advised many companies, ranging from start-ups to multinationals, on their sustainability performance and reporting, especially through stakeholder panels and advisory boards. As well, she has been an active member of several committees that work to improve sustainability performance and has won numerous awards for her leadership in implementing sustainability projects. In her spare time, she is an avid outdoors person and enjoys engaging with the natural environment.

Index

Accountability, 22, 32, 48, 62, 116
Accurate, 34, 94, 100–101, 109, 113, 126
Achievable, 79
Aggregated data, 105–106
Air France KLM, 118
Alma Media, 97–98
Apple, 112
ASICS, 41–44
Assurance, 34, 44, 108–110, 125, 127
    auditing guidelines/standards, 123–124
    confidence, 110–112
    defined, 111
    independence, 123
    internal controls and internal audits, 113–118
    internal vs. external, 112–113
    limited and reasonable, 119, 121, 122, 125–127
    provider and expertise, 121–122
    scope, 124–125
    third-party assurance, 118–126
    third-party commentary, 119, 126–127
Assurance engagement, 119–120, 124
Assurance statement, 34, 111, 119–121, 126, 128
Auditing guidelines/standards, 123–124

Balance, 4, 22, 84, 95, 98–100
Bank of America, 79–80
Baxter, 86
Beinhocker, E., 7, 68
Benchmark, 79, 88, 101–103
Benefit Corporation, 8
Bhopal gas leak (1984), 25
BHP, 58, 59
Board of directors, 42, 61, 82, 101, 110, 113, 117
Braam, G., 126

Brundtland report, 11, 12, 20, 25

Canon, 75, 76
Capability, 61, 62, 65–68, 79, 115, 117
Capitalism, 1–4, 7, 21, 68
Carbon Disclosure Project (CDP), 32, 33, 44, 104, 136
Careless illustrations, 105
Carson, R., 10, 11
CDP. *See* Carbon Disclosure Project
CDSB. *See* Climate Disclosure Standards Board
CERES. *See* Coalition for Environmentally Responsible Economies
Certain subject matter, 113, 117
Clear and specific disclosure, 106–107
Climate change, 31–32, 47, 78
Climate Disclosure Standards Board (CDSB), 32, 33
Coalition for Environmentally Responsible Economies (CERES), 26, 28
Commitment, 61–65, 67, 68, 115, 117
Comparability, 101–103
Comparable, 77, 101, 104
Complete, 96–98, 121, 136
Comply vs. innovate, 67–68
Conclusion, 120
Confidence, 110–112
Conflict minerals, 47, 138
ConocoPhillips, 115, 116
Control system, 43, 115
Corporate Reporting Dialogue, 32–37, 138
Corporate Responsibility Committee, 63, 64
Corporate social responsibility (CSR), 49
Cost-benefit principle, 138

INDEX

Cost effective, 86
Credibility, 34, 36, 77, 92, 94, 96–107, 109, 122
Credible reporting, 91–92
  accuracy and reliability, 100–101
  aggregated data, 105–106
  balance, 98–100
  careless illustrations, 105
  characteristics, 94–96
  comparability, 101–103
  completeness, 97–98
  guidelines and standards, 103–104
  imprecise and vague disclosure, 106–107
  trust, 92–94
Customers, 50

Decision making, 4, 22–24, 31, 59, 64, 77, 80, 110
Dell, 73
Diversity, 44
Domtar Corporation, 99, 100
Dow Jones Sustainability Index (DJSI), 36

Eco-efficiency indicators, 88–89
Economic, 3–5, 7–10, 13, 22, 44, 68, 81–85, 88
  dimension, 5
  emphasis, 9
  indicators, 82
Edelman Trust Barometer, 93
Effectiveness indicators, 85–87
Efficiency, 69
Efficiency indicators, 85–87
Employees, 50
Environment, 3, 10, 13, 25, 44, 88, 93
Environmental dimension, 5, 10
Environmental indicators, 82
Environmental management system (EMS), 41
Environmental reporting, 32
Environmental, social, and governance (ESG), 36, 37, 82
External assurance, 112–113, 118–119, 122, 126
Exxon Valdez oil spill (1989), 26

Faithful representation, 111
Financial Accounting Standards Board (FASB), 33
Financial performance reporting, 22, 24
Financial reporting, 95–96
Five capitals and value creation, 16–19
5 Ps model, 16, 19
Formal system, 60

Generally Accepted Accounting Principles (GAAP), 27
GHG emissions, 75, 78, 88, 89, 104, 117
Gide, A., 40
Global Reporting Initiative (GRI), 28, 29, 31, 33, 34, 44, 48–49, 75, 78, 95–98, 103, 118
Governments, 50
Greenhouse gas (GHG) emissions, 104
Greenwashing, 93, 98
GRI. *See* Global Reporting Initiative
GRI Sector Disclosures, 143
Guidelines, 25, 27–32, 59–60, 111, 123–124, 137–139
  and standards, 103–104

Hanauer, N., 7, 68

Iberdrola, 137
IIRC. *See* International Integrated Reporting Council
Impact indicator, 82
Imprecise and vague disclosure, 106–107
Independence, 123
Independent assurance provider, 119–121
Indicators, 8, 27, 31, 43–44, 71–72, 91, 97, 109–111, 118, 124–126
  characteristics, 77–81
  classification, 81
  eco-efficiency/socioeconomic, 88–89

economic, environmental, and social, 81–85
efficiency and effectiveness, 85–87
leading and lagging, 87–88
to policy, 74–76
quantitative vs. qualitative disclosure, 72–74
Informal system, 60
Input, 47, 81–87, 109
Integrated report/reporting (IR), 29–31, 44, 92, 135
Intel, 65–67
Internal assurance, 112–118
Internal audit, 112–119
Internal audit department (function), 113
Internal auditor, 101, 113, 116–118
Internal controls, 112–118
International Accounting Standards Board (IASB), 33, 96
International Financial Reporting Standards (IFRS), 27, 96
International Integrated Reporting Council (IIRC), 17, 29–30, 33
International Organization for Standardization (ISO), 33, 58–60, 107
International Standard on Assurance Engagements, 119
ISO. *See* International Organization for Standardization
ISO 14000, 58
ISO 14001, 59
ISO 26000, 59

Kramer, M. R., 68

Lagging indicators, 83, 87–88
Leading indicators, 81, 87–88
Legitimacy theory, 8
Legitimate, 9, 11, 22
Limited assurance, 121, 122, 125, 127
Local communities, 50

Management Discussion and Analysis (MD&A), 73

Management systems, 43, 91, 109, 111, 114, 115
approach, 57–58
commitment and capability, 61–70
formal and informal systems, 60
standards, 58–60
Marks and Spencer (M&S), 99, 101, 102
Marriott International, 83
Material, 31, 42, 44, 47–49, 77, 96, 97
Materiality, 96, 98
Materiality matrix, 42, 49–51
Measurability indicator, 83–88
Measurable, 78
Microsoft, 65
Millennium development goals (MDGs), 13–14, 16, 19, 29
Multi-stakeholder process, 28, 41, 42, 58, 64, 75, 109

Nested circles, 13, 19
NGOs, CSR councils, specialized institutions, 49
Nike, 64, 116

Objective, 42–44, 49, 66–68, 85, 86, 113, 123
Off-the-shelf vs. customized policies, 46–47
Operational organizational level, 62
Organizational commitment and capability, 61–70
Organizational sustainability, 40–44, 132–135
Organization for Economic Co-operation and Development (OECD), 25
Outcome, 7, 18, 82–88, 111
Outotec, 127
Output, 18, 81–88

Peeters, R., 126
Performance, 12, 34, 40, 41, 43–44, 57, 79, 84, 91–93, 97, 99, 100, 102, 103, 109–113, 116, 126. *See also* Indicators

Performance and Disclosure
    Committee, 64
Performance indicators, 83, 84
Performance measurement system,
    71–72, 81, 91
Policy, 42, 44–54
    indicators to, 74–76
Porritt, J., 17
Porter, M. E., 68
Practitioner, 119
Primary stakeholder, 6, 23
Principles of Responsible Investing
    (PRI), 37
Priority of humans vs. nature, 46
Public Environmental Reporting
    Initiative (PERI), 27, 29

Quaker Oats, 11
Quantitative vs. qualitative disclosure,
    72–74

Reasonable assurance, 119, 121, 122,
    124–127
Regulator, 6, 24
Relevant, 80
Reliability, 100–101
Reporting. *See also* Credible reporting;
    Sustainability reporting
    organization, 75, 123, 139
Rio Earth Summit, 12
Risk strategy, 32, 34, 43, 49

SAM, 36
Samsung
    internal assurances, 114
    and stakeholder engagement,
        49–50
    working hours benchmark, 101,
        102
SASB. *See* Sustainability Accounting
    Standards Board
Schneider Electric, 80
Secondary stakeholder, 6, 7, 24, 32,
    34
Securities Exchange Commission
    (SEC), 138
Self- vs. community interest, 46

Selling general and administrative
    expenses, 105
Shareholder, 3, 4, 6, 8, 23, 37, 44, 54
Shareholders & investors, 50
Shell, 24
Short-term vs. long-term thinking, 46
Social, 3, 5, 9–12, 27, 81–85, 88
Social dimension, 5, 10–12
Social indicators, 82
Social license, 8, 9, 22
Socioeconomic indicators, 88–89
Specific, 77–79
Specific, Measurable, Achievable,
    Relevant, and Timely
    (SMART), 77–81
Spin, 93–94
Stakeholder engagement, 45, 47–50,
    52, 53, 74, 80, 91, 97
Stakeholders, 6–8, 42, 45, 47–48, 92
Starbucks, 69–70
Strategic organizational level, 62
Subject matter information, 120
Suncor Energy Inc, 106
Suppliers, 49
Sustainability, 2–5
    assurances (*See* Assurance)
    capitalism, 1–4, 7, 21, 68
    commitment and capability, 61–70
    dimensions, 3, 5
    evolution of, 8–12
    and financial reporting, 95–96
    formal and informal systems, 60
    management systems, 58–60 (*See
        also* Management systems)
    models, 12–20
    organizational model, 40–44,
        132–135
    performance measurement, 71–72
    reports and reporting, 137–138
    and stakeholders, 2–8, 44–54
    systems approach, 57–58
Sustainability Accounting
    Standards Board (SASB), 31,
    33, 38, 75
Sustainability management system
    (SMS), 41
Sustainability performance, 24, 29,
    39, 72, 93, 97, 131

INDEX

Sustainability reporting, 34, 41, 44, 49–51, 66, 72–75, 83, 85, 91–99, 101, 103, 104, 134, 138–140
   assurances (*See* Assurance)
   corporate reporting dialogue, 32–37
   evolution of, 24–26, 35
   and financial reporting, 95–96
   guidelines, 27–32
   plethora of, 135–136
   progress, 21–24
Sustainable capitalism, 2, 4, 7
Sustainable Development Goals (SDGs), 14–16, 19, 20, 29, 72

Tactical organizational level, 62
Task Force on Climate-related Financial Disclosures (TFCD), 32, 75
Teck's materiality matrix, 50–51, 96–97
Third-party assurance, 118–126
Third-party commentary, 119, 126–127

3Ps (profits, planet, and people), 3
Timely, 80
Transparent, 8, 25, 36, 38, 49, 50
Trust, 92–94

Unbiased party, 123
Unilever, 16

Vague and imprecise disclosure, 106–107
Value creation capitals model, 16–18
Values orientation, 45
Venn diagram, 3–4, 12, 19

Wells Fargo & Company, 63
World Business Council for Sustainable Development (WBCSD), 89
World Commission on Environment and Development (WCED), 11, 12, 25

XBRL (eXtensible Business Reporting Language), 103

OTHER TITLES IN THE FINANCIAL ACCOUNTING, AUDITING, AND TAXATION COLLECTION

Mark Bettner, Bucknell University and Michael Coyne, Fairfield University, Editor

- *Applications of Accounting Information Systems* by David M. Shapiro
- *A Non-Technical Guide to International Accounting* by Roger Hussey and Audra Ong
- *Forensic Accounting and Financial Statement Fraud, Volume I* by Zabihollah Rezaee
- *Forensic Accounting and Financial Statement Fraud, Volume II* by Zabi Rezaee
- *The Tax Aspects of Acquiring a Business, Second Edition* by Seago W. Eugene
- *The Story Underlying the Numbers* by Iyer S. Veena
- *Pick a Number, Second Edition* by Roger Hussey and Audra Ong
- *Using Accounting & Financial Information, Second Edition* by Mark S. Bettner
- *Corporate Governance in the Aftermath of the Financial Crisis, Volume IV* by Zabihollah Rezaee
- *Corporate Governance in the Aftermath of the Financial Crisis, Volume III* by Zabihollah Rezaee

Announcing the Business Expert Press Digital Library

Concise e-books business students need for classroom and research

This book can also be purchased in an e-book collection by your library as

- a one-time purchase,
- that is owned forever,
- allows for simultaneous readers,
- has no restrictions on printing, and
- can be downloaded as PDFs from within the library community.

Our digital library collections are a great solution to beat the rising cost of textbooks. E-books can be loaded into their course management systems or onto students' e-book readers.
The **Business Expert Press** digital libraries are very affordable, with no obligation to buy in future years. For more information, please visit **www.businessexpertpress.com/librarians**. To set up a trial in the United States, please email **sales@businessexpertpress.com**.

CPSIA information can be obtained
at www.ICGtesting.com
Printed in the USA
BVHW010320250322
632204BV00008B/746